CW01648758

CATALOGUE OF AN EXHIBITION OF POTTERY
HANNAH BARLOW
A PIONEER DOULTON ARTIST
1851 — 1916

with
The Life & Work of Hannah Barlow
by Peter Rose

Arranged by
CHRISTIE'S
and held at
85, Old Brompton Road, South Kensington, London, S.W.7.

on
Tuesday 6th — Saturday 10th August 1985, 10 a.m.

Published by
RICHARD DENNIS
144 Kensington Church Street
London W8 4BN

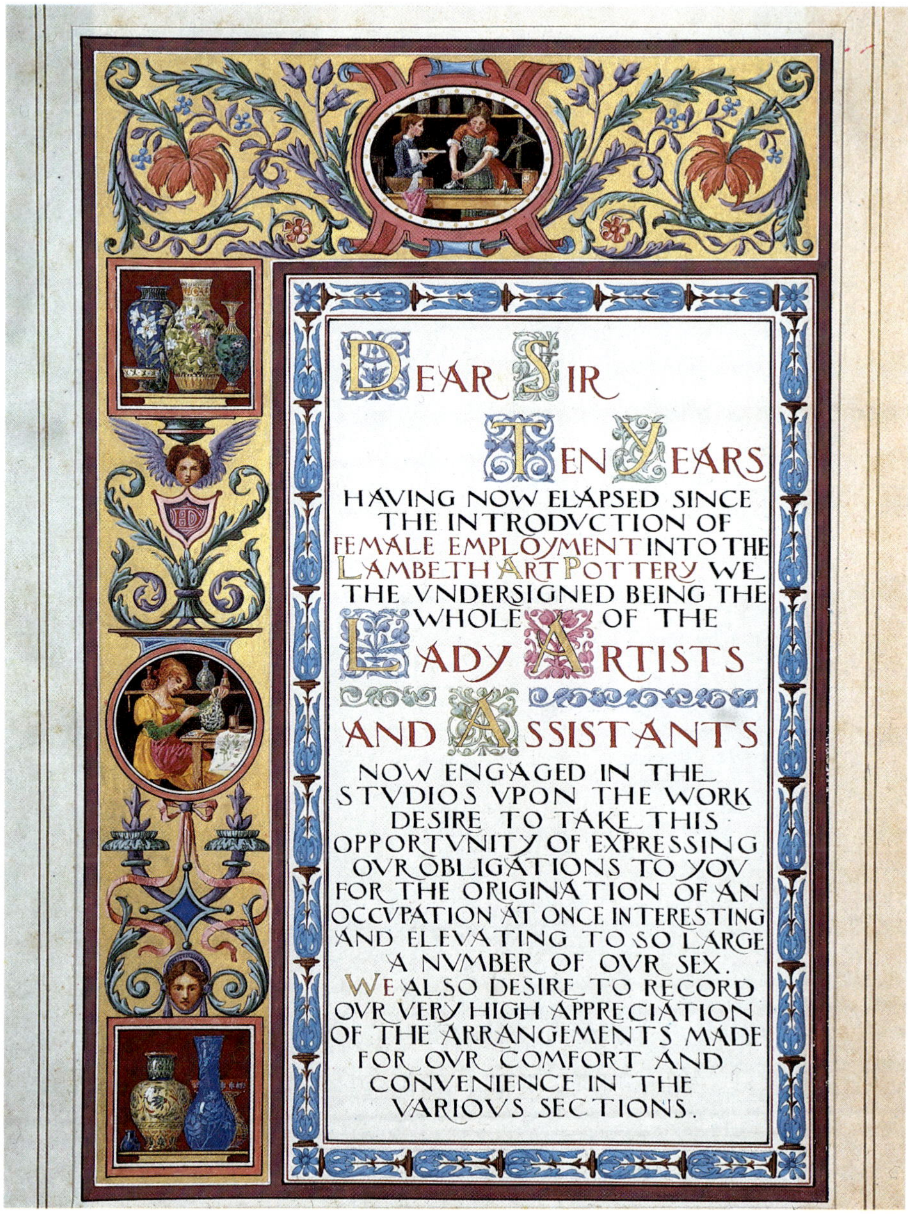

DEAR SIR

TEN YEARS

HAVING NOW ELAPSED SINCE
THE INTRODVCTION OF
FEMALE EMPLOYMENT INTO THE
LAMBETH ART POTTERY WE
THE VNDERSIGNED BEING THE
WHOLE OF THE

LADY ARTISTS

AND ASSISTANTS

NOW ENGAGED IN THE
STVDIOS VPON THE WORK
DESIRE TO TAKE THIS
OPPORTVNITY OF EXPRESSING
OVR OBLIGATIONS TO YOV
FOR THE ORIGINATION OF AN
OCCVPATION AT ONCE INTERESTING
AND ELEVATING TO SO LARGE
A NVMBER OF OVR SEX.
WE ALSO DESIRE TO RECORD
OVR VERY HIGH APPRECIATION
OF THE ARRANGEMENTS MADE
FOR OVR COMFORT AND
CONVENIENCE IN THE
VARIOVS SECTIONS.

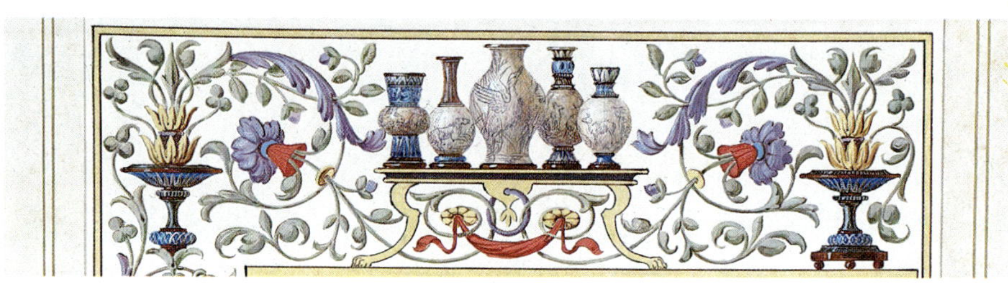

Pages from the manuscript presented to Henry Doulton in 1881/2 by the lady artists and assistants at Lambeth, the second showing a vignette of Hannah Barlow pots above artists' signatures. Reproduced with the courtesy of The Minet Branch Library of the London Borough of Lambeth.

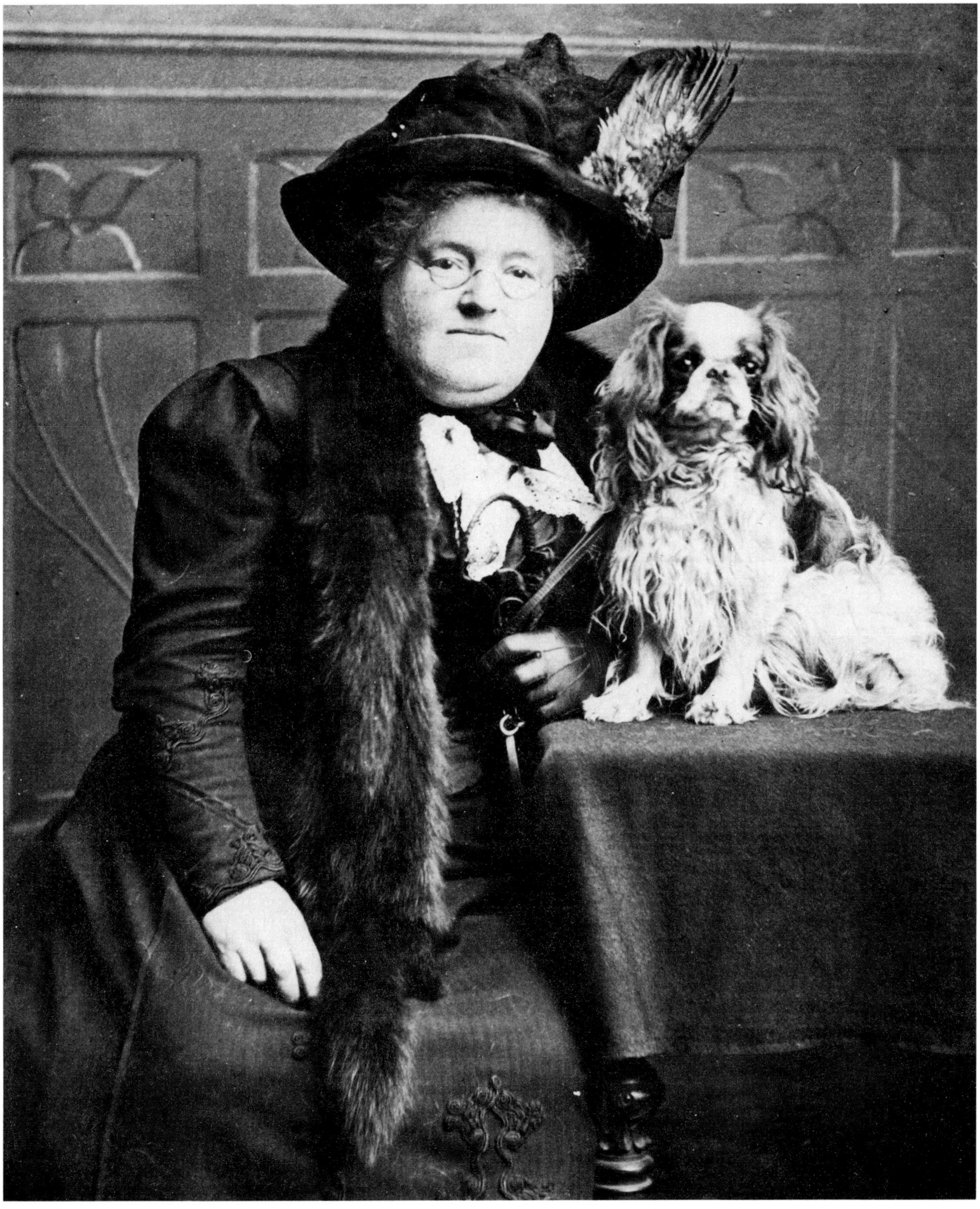

Hannah B. Barlow & Rufus Darwin, February 1913.

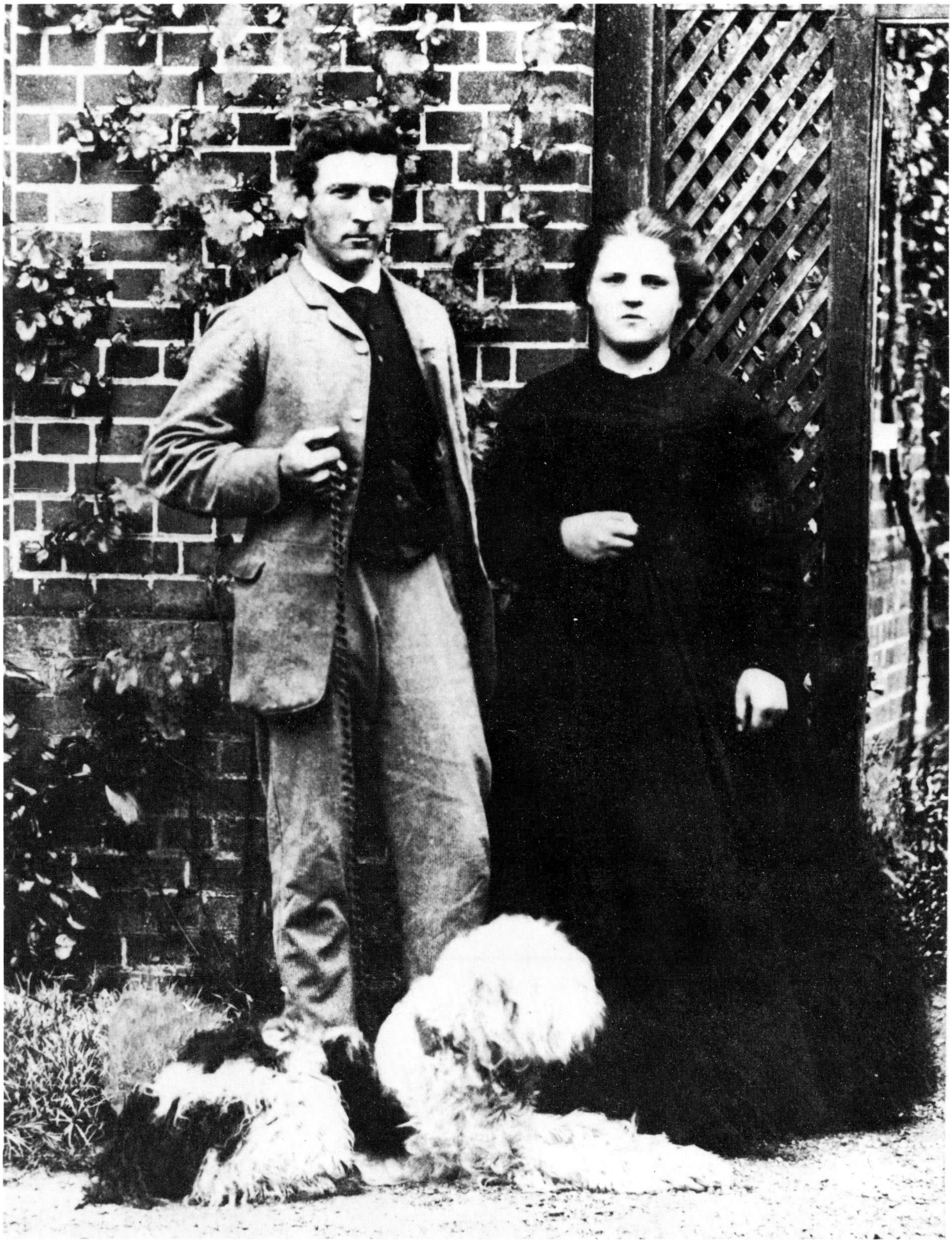

Figure 1: Irlam and Hannah Barlow, probably at the Grange, 1867.

THE LIFE AND WORK OF HANNAH BARLOW

1. CHILDHOOD

Hannah Bolton Barlow, a spinster lady of decidedly genteel origins and upbringing, decorated many thousands of pieces of pottery each to her individual design. She also helped to pioneer one of the most remarkable nineteenth century artistic and social experiments in the employment of women in the previously exclusively male preserve of the Lambeth potteries.

A tragic change in her family circumstances precipitated Hannah Barlow's career as an Art Pottery decorator. At the age of sixteen she unexpectedly found herself obliged to earn her own living: she moved away from her home to Vauxhall in South London and began to attend John Sparkes' Lambeth School of Art. A year or so later she was joined by her brother Arthur and in 1873 by her sister Florence. All three were soon working in the newly established Art Pottery studios of Doulton & Co.

It was in 1842 that Hannah's father, Benjamin Irlam Barlow, a young man of 29 years, was appointed Bank Manager at Bishop's Stortford and began to raise his large family of sons and daughters. Charles Edward the eldest was followed by Alice Jane and then by Arthur Bolton and Benjamin Irlam (called Irlam by the family). Three daughters followed: Frances Louisa, Lucy Anna and Hannah Bolton. Another son, Hubert John, and the youngest daughter, Florence Elizabeth, completed the family. All nine children survived the hazardous process of growing up in a Victorian world where the vicissitudes of accident and disease took their toll in even the most affluent families; although even in their country paradise the Barlow children did eventually experience incurable illness and sudden death to mar their otherwise idyllic upbringing.

Hannah was born in 1851, the year of the Great Exhibition and a pivotal point in the shift of taste which created the reformist art movements of the sixties and seventies. The earlier part of her childhood was spent in the rich agricultural countryside of Hertfordshire. During the fifties the prosperity of the Barlow family increased enabling them to move from their relatively modest establishment at Little Hadham, situated about three miles west of Bishop's Stortford, to the Grange, a substantial estate at Hatfield Broad Oak, Essex, about five miles south-west of the town.

The childhood of the large family of Barlow siblings is eloquently and movingly described by Hannah's mother, also named Hannah, a virtuous Quaker lady of cultivated, artistic tastes, in a memoir she wrote about her son Arthur.[1] Although her husband Benjamin was Church of England and "warmly attached to its doctrines . . . (he was) liberal and tolerant with regard to the religious convictions of others."[2] In consequence of Mrs Barlow's own views none of the children was baptised, indeed a sort of nature worship permeated the household.

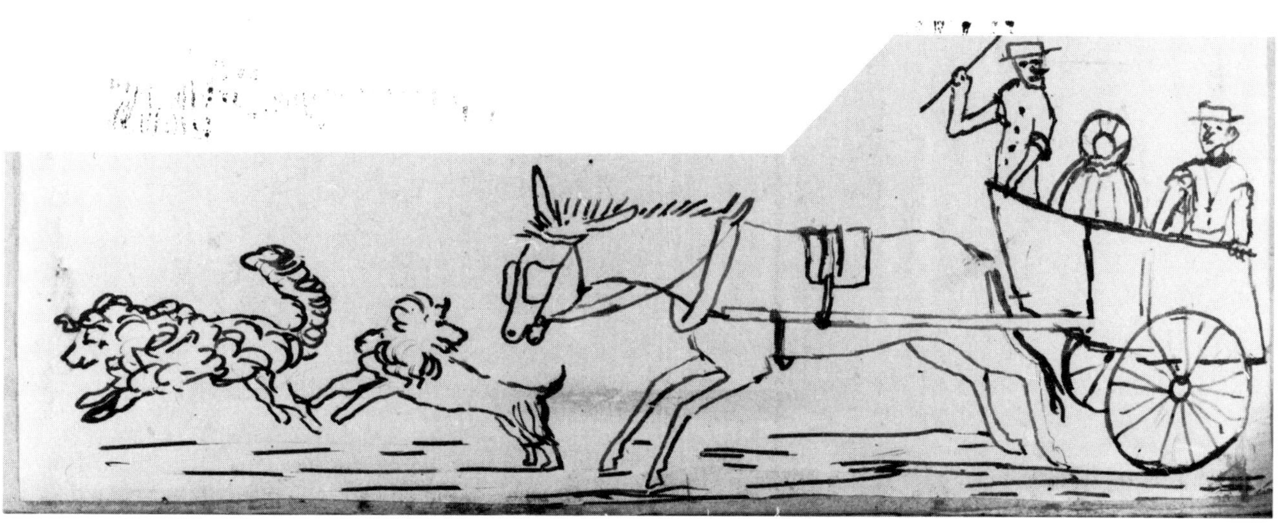

Figure 2: Sketch of the Barlow children by Irlam Barlow, c. 1865.

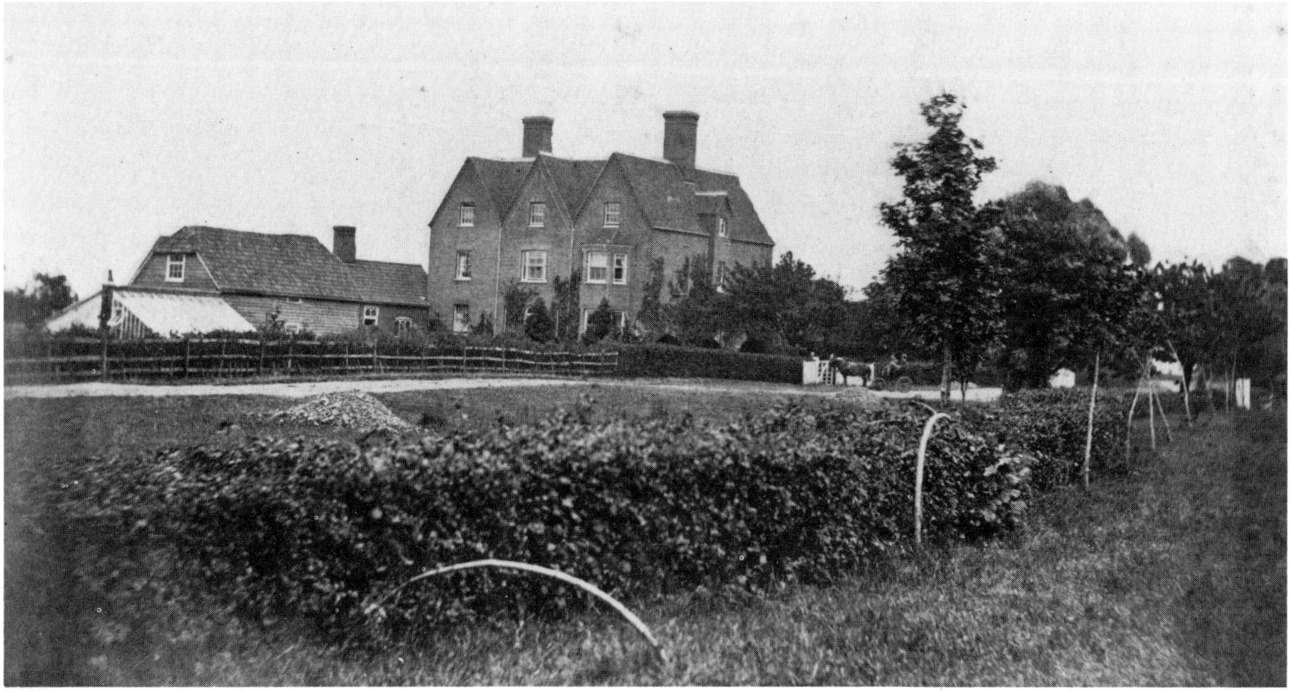

Figure 3: "The Grange", Hatfield, Essex: childhood home of Hannah Barlow.

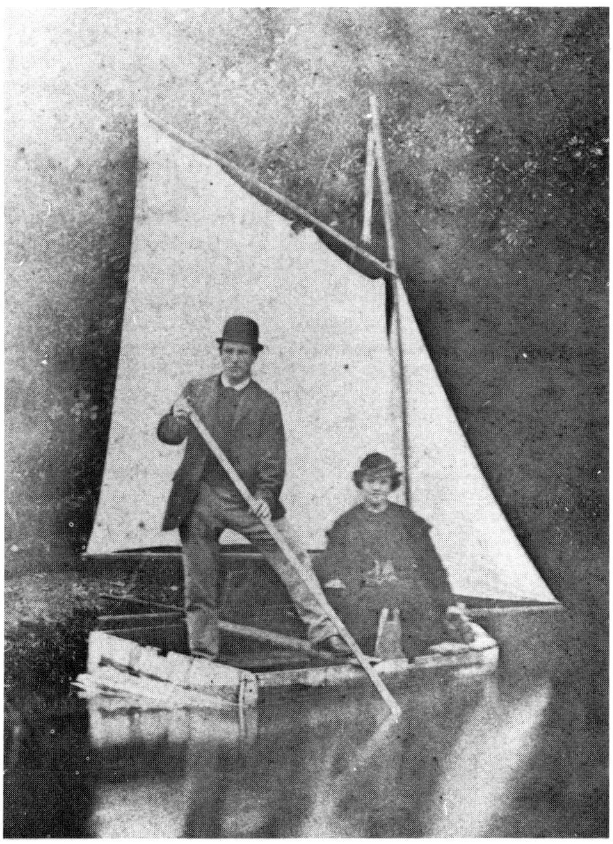

Figure 4: Irlam and Hannah Barlow on the moat at the Grange, August 1867.

Benjamin Barlow had a "decided preference for the pursuits and surroundings of country life, fondness for animals, taste for the cultivation of land, and desire that all his children should be thoroughly imbued with a love of nature."[3] It was in order to satisfy these preferences more fully that he decided to move the family to the Grange set in 250 acres of agricultural land, but still within easy reach of the Bank at Bishop's Stortford. The house was a three gabled affair on three floors, built in an unpretentious Georgian style (Figure 3). With its barnlike outbuildings and lean-to greenhouses it has the air of a traditional farmhouse rather than a gentleman's residence, but it was no doubt more than adequately commodious for such a large family. Its modest appearance may perhaps be deceptive for there is mention of a "long gallery surrounding the hall (with) several rooms on the same level",[4] suggesting at least a touch of grandeur.

The move to the Grange in 1859 coincided with the first of the major misfortunes which afflicted the family. Arthur Barlow then aged thirteen was stricken with acute inflammation of the hip-joint, supposedly the result of an injury received in playing with his schoolfellows. The condition baffled the local family doctor Mr Hodson, who, without such modern aids as X-rays and anti-biotics, was unable to diagnose or treat effectively the rapidly worsening condition, which soon became chronic. Until his death twenty years later Arthur Barlow remained a cripple, at best only able to hobble on crutches and in constant pain.

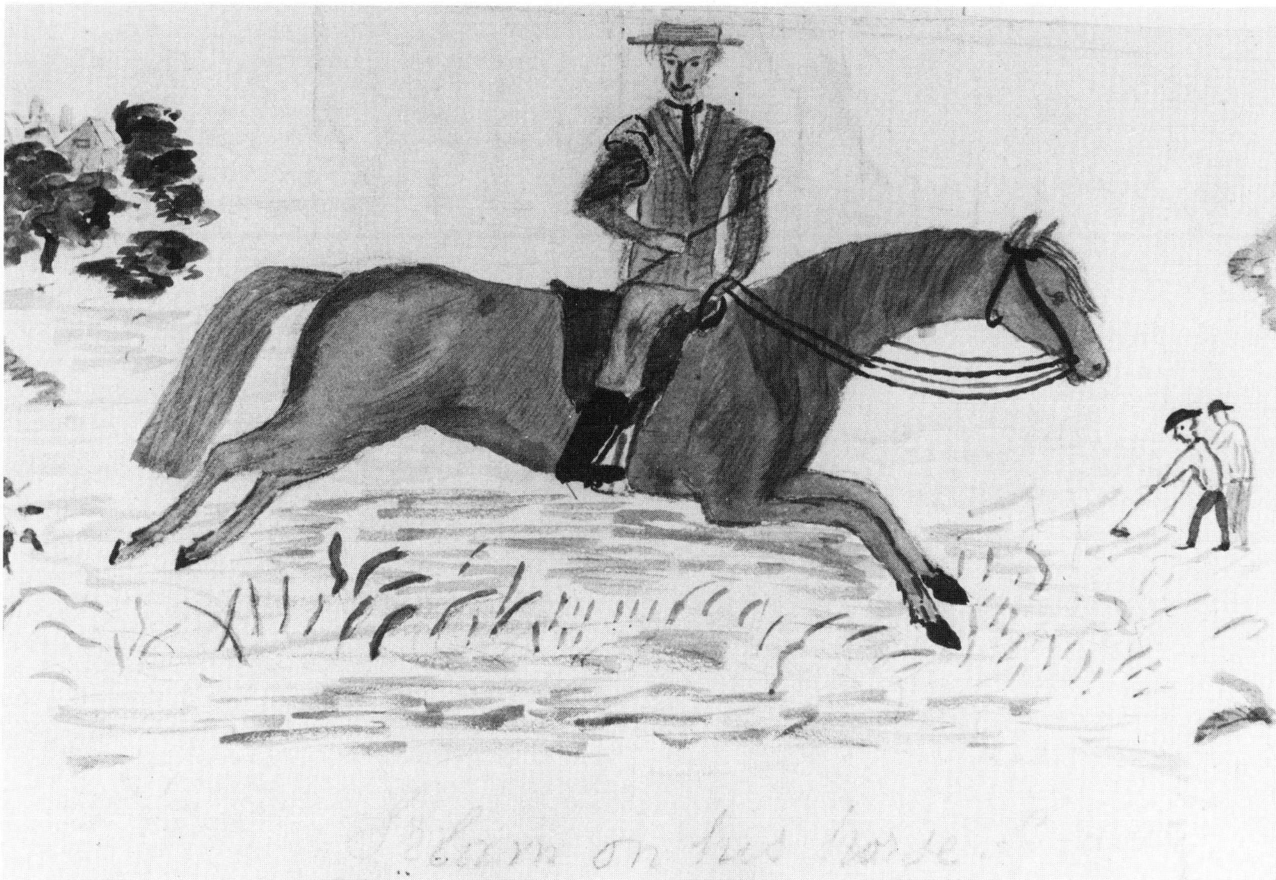

Figure 5: "Irlam on his horse, Beauty", by Hannah Barlow, 1866.

His mother and sisters cared for him and Hannah in particular played a crucial role in assisting him in his work at Doulton's.

The Grange was so secluded that the family was able to live in a world of their own. Surrounded by land which they owned and cultivated, it fully satisfied Benjamin Barlow's passion for laying out, planting and generally improving the property; the estate was teeming with animal and bird life, domestic and otherwise. There were horses and ponies, peafowl, pigeons and other fancy poultry and "scarcely any restriction as to the number or variety of pet birds and animals."[5] A childhood sketch by Hannah shows her brother Irlam riding a horse with the distinctive gables of the Grange in the distance (Figure 5). The children in their country pursuits were often accompanied by a colourful array of ill-assorted creatures all apparently living in mutual harmony and accord. Arthur, although confined to an invalid carriage, shared in their pleasures:

"Sometimes his brothers and sisters would take him long distances in the fields and lanes, often with a considerable addition to the party in the company of an odd variety of pets — several dogs, a pet lamb, a tame jackdaw, and a remarkably sociable partridge. The latter bird had been hatched and brought up by a common barn-door fowl, and although at perfect liberty was for three years surprisingly tame and familiar. It would run by the side of Arthur's carriage

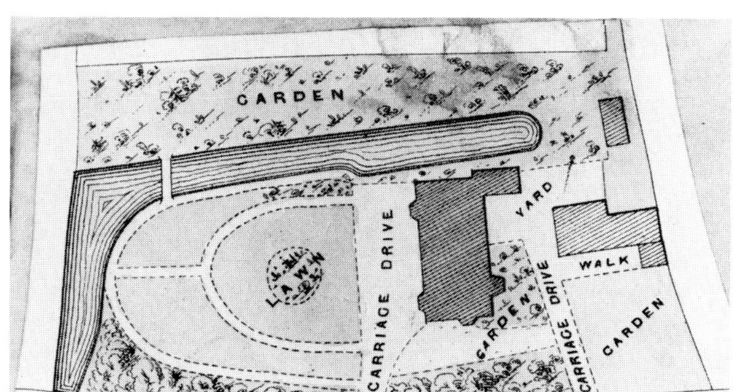

Figure 6: Plan of the Grange.

for miles, sometimes flying up to sit on his hand or nestle beside him; a little Skye terrier was generally one of the party, and although accustomed to going out with its master in pursuit of game, and very clever in finding and bringing to him a wounded partridge. Floss was always on friendly terms with the tame one, as were also the larger dogs and other domestic animals, though the partridge was very pugnacious and would often audaciously presume upon their forbearance. The jackdaw would perch on the axle-tree of the carriage, now and then descending to look about it, or flitting along the road for a change."[6]

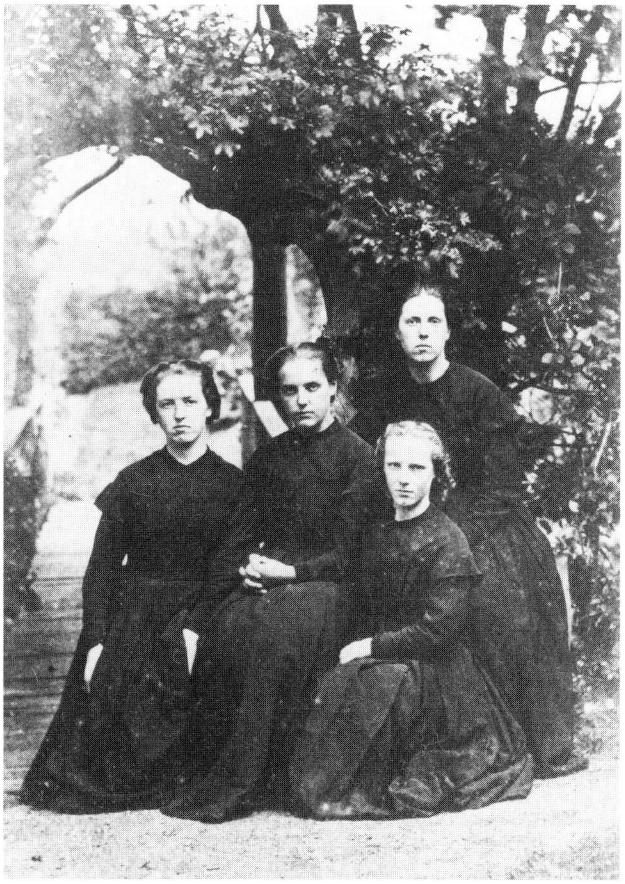

Figure 7: Alice Jane, Frances, Lucy and Florence Barlow 'Near bridge at the Grange', 1867.

2. EARNING A LIVING

The family idyll was abruptly shattered when in December 1866 Benjamin Barlow died. It was both sudden and unexpected for he was in his early fifties with his schemes and plans for the Grange still unfulfilled. Within a year the house had been sold and his widow and children were facing an uncertain and financially straightened future. They moved to Dunmow Road Cottage in the neighbourhood of Bishop's Stortford, which remained Mrs Barlow's home for several years. A sketchbook[7] drawing by Hannah "Waiting to be fed" (Figure 8) dated September 1872 shows a corner of the cottage garden with the household dog and cat contentedly sharing territory with goats, pigeons and a miscellany of cocks and hens. This unlikely coterie is perhaps the nucleus of Hannah's small private zoo at Wraysbury near Staines, which contemporary accounts describe.[8]

Fortunately two of the three older boys were mature enough to fend for themselves. Charles and Irlam were each married and moved to Lancashire and Stratford respectively, thus relieving Mrs Barlow of a small portion of her cares. Arthur, the younger son Hubert, and the five daughters, remained however, and the question of careers for them became a matter of great urgency. Arthur had been encouraged to take up woodcarving as a therapy by Mr Hodson (Figure 9) the family doctor and, lying on his side, with only a few elementary tools at his disposal, he laboriously worked on simple tasks such as decorative bread-boards. He was completely untutored until a sculptor friend of the family, W.G. Rogers (Figure 10) took an interest and provided specimens of carving. He was even able to enlist the support of the great critic John Ruskin who, with characteristic kindness, wrote a letter of encouragement and advice to the young man. Arthur delighted in naturalistically detailed carving, particularly of plants and flowers, cutting directly into the wood without any preliminary sketches. Mrs Barlow's first instinct was to offer these carvings to "wealthy individuals"[10] rather than submit the invalid to the restrictions and anxiety of taking "orders".

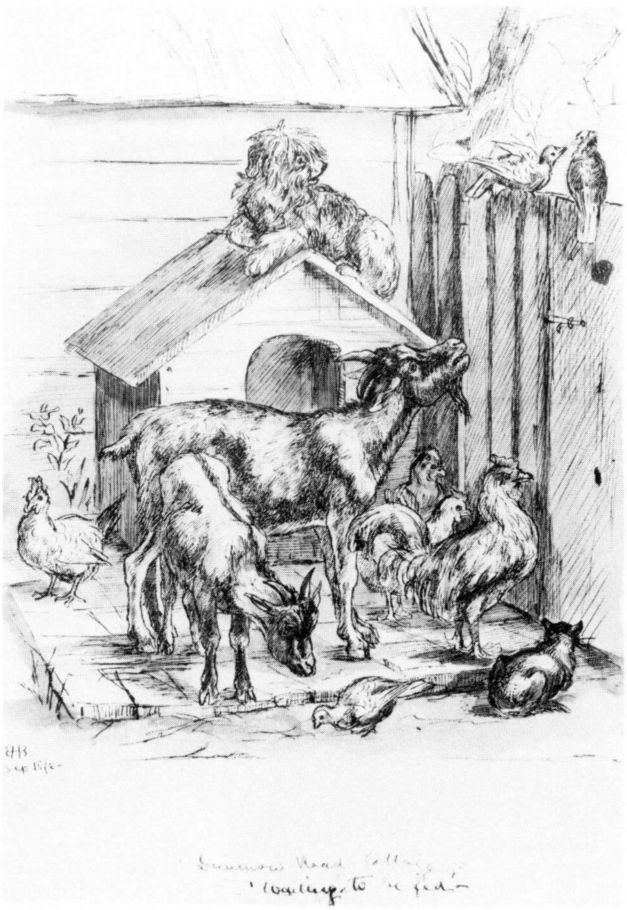

Figure 8: "Waiting to be Fed", by Hannah Barlow, 1872.

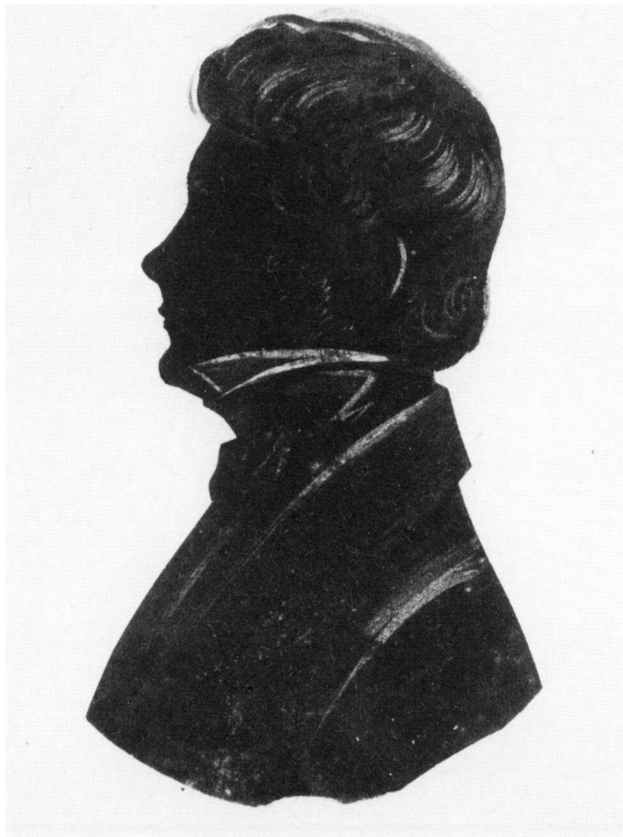

Figure 9: Dr. Thomas B. Hodson, family doctor who attended Arthur after his accident.

Another solution to the problem of Arthur's career

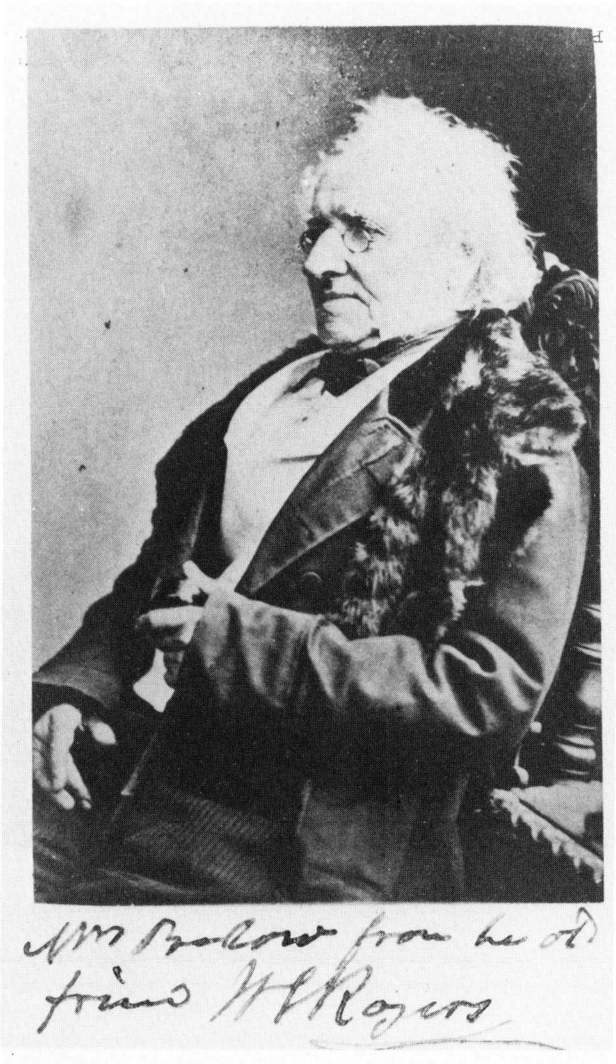

Figure 10: W.G. Rogers, wood carver & sculptor, tutor to Arthur Barlow, c. 1870.

fortunately presented itself, involving Hannah's own career, before Mrs Barlow's impractical enterprise was launched. As a child Hannah Barlow's love of animals had found expression in sketches and watercolours which are full of life and vigour although she was untrained. In early childhood she had watched an itinerant potter working on his portable wheel, raising and shaping jugs and vases from the crude clay. The memory of that seemingly magical transformation remained with her. After being introduced by John Sparkes (Figure 11) headmaster of Lambeth School of Art, by a young friend of hers, Edith Rogers, she decided to enrol as a student.

The School had been founded in 1854 by Canon Gregory to enable "the parishioners of Lambeth to obtain an elementary knowledge of design."[11] It formed part of the government initiated expansion of design education aimed at improving the design quality of manufactured goods. Its first headmaster John C.L. Sparkes was an enlightened, energetic and farsighted man who saw the need for the Design Schools to forge close links with industry. In the locality of Lambeth the pottery industry was pre-eminent and in particular the firm of Doulton and Co., was rapidly expanding under the dynamic direction of Henry Doulton, son of the founder of the firm John Doulton. Together with a mutual friend, Edward

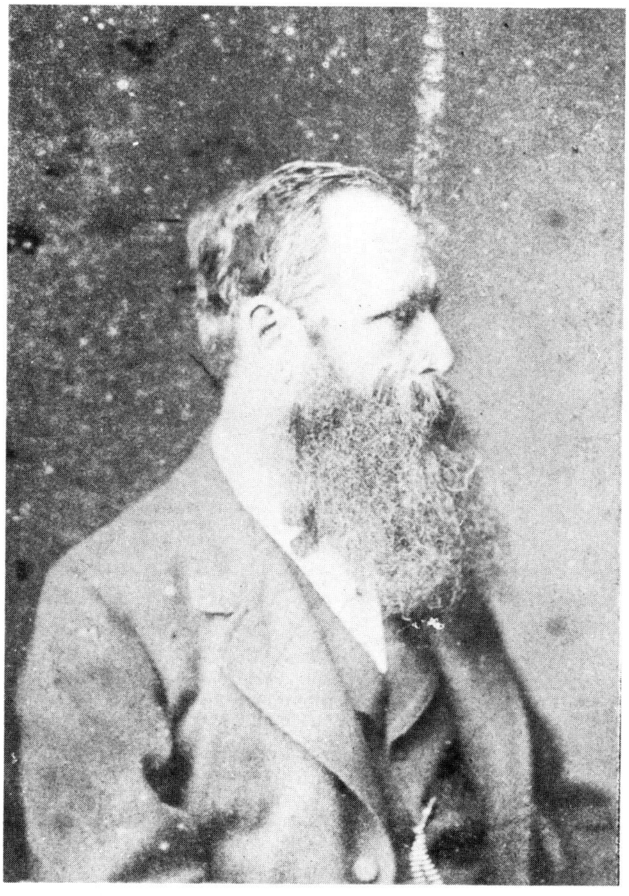

Figure 11: John C.L. Sparkes, headmaster of Lambeth School of Art, c. 1876.

Cresy, Sparkes persuaded Henry Doulton to experiment with a revival of the salt-glaze Grès de Flandres ware. That enterprise eventually gave employment to many hundreds of students from Sparkes's school. The first tentative start, however, was made early in 1867 when the young George Tinworth[12] was offered employment in modelling terra-cotta reliefs, water filters and other utilitarian products for the firm.

One unexpected and, in some eyes, unwelcome outcome of the expansion in publicly financed art education was the large number of young ladies who enrolled. The intention was to train young men from the working and artisan classes for employment as skilled workmen and designers in industry and commerce, but not to provide an art education of a more general and non-vocational kind. From the start controversy raged over such activities as life drawing, creating original work rather than copying and so on. The young ladies who were attracted to the schools tended to come from a higher social class than their male counterparts and to be seeking that more general education already under attack for its subversive influence on the young men. In addition these young ladies were only too liable to get married soon after completing their courses, which, according to the accepted practice of the time, meant giving up employment.[13] It was consequently of the greatest importance for John Sparkes not only to find employment for the men students locally but also to seek congenial openings for the women.

Early in 1868, a few months after the move to Dunmow Road Cottage, Hannah began her studies at Lambeth School of Art. She stayed with family friends, very probably the Rogers, at 48 South Lambeth Road, Vauxhall. A year later Arthur, whose health had improved somewhat, joined her. For the next ten years their careers were closely linked, although their individual styles of work developed differently. Arthur mainly studied modelling, developing a formalised style of decoration described in enthusiastic terms by John Sparkes:

"He took an entirely different line from that followed by his sister. His ornament is original — a flowing, tumbling wealth of vegetable form wreaths around the jug, now and then fixed by a bow, or pinned down by a point of modelled form . . . His good taste and perfect mechanical ingenuity have carried his art into fields of decoration of unexpected beauty."[14]

Hannah's studies took an intensely active course, working directly in her sketchbooks with pen and pencil, seizing every opportunity to draw animals and birds either observed directly or from memory. She was frequently out in Bushy Park, Teddington, visiting the cattle show at Windsor, the dog show at Crystal Palace, Thorley Rectory, Wraysbury and of course Dunmow Road Cottage. Her sketchbooks contain hundreds of studies showing variable quality and finish, but each is imbued with enthusiasm, vigour and an all-pervading love of animals. Sparkes made the following comments about her style:

"Miss Barlow's quick sketches of animals show an intense feeling for the spirit of the beasts and birds represented. These etched out figures are, so to speak, instantaneous photographs of the creatures. She possesses a certain Japanese facility of representing the largest amount of fact in the fewest lines, all correct, and all embodying in a high degree the essential character of her subject."[15]

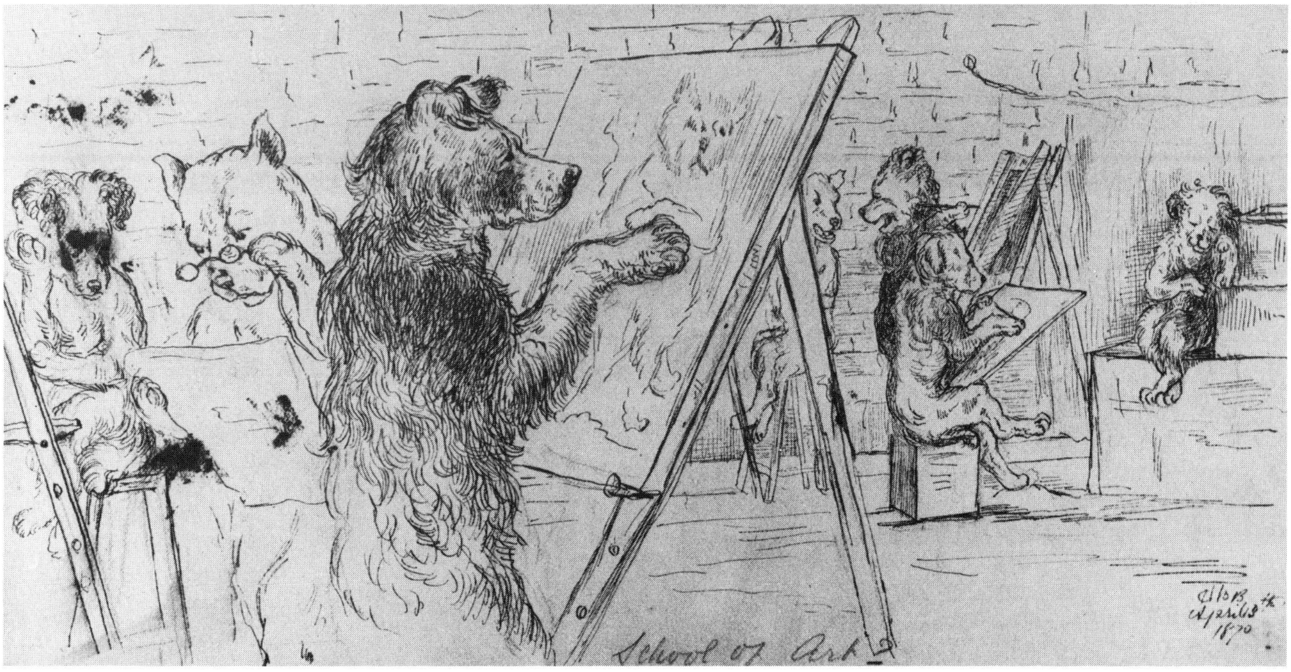

Figure 12: "School of Art", by Hannah Barlow, 1870.

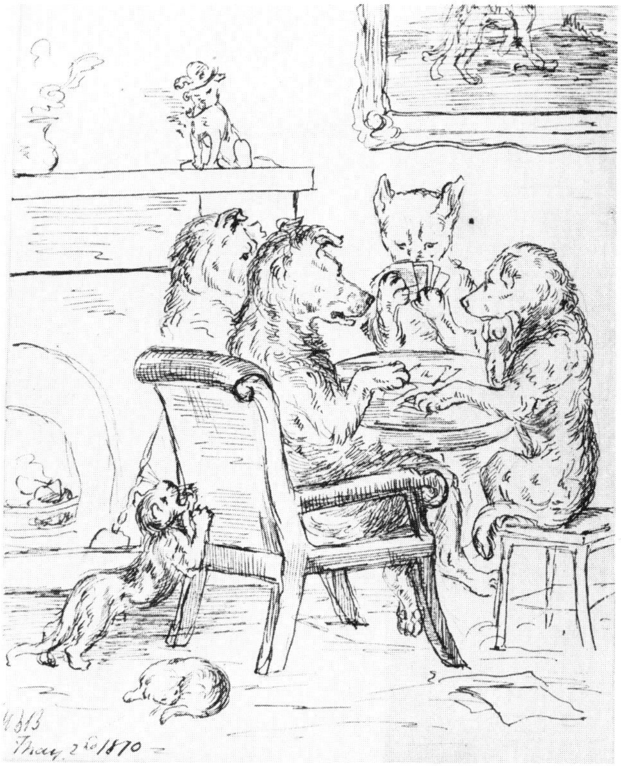

Figure 13: The dog card game, by Hannah Barlow, 1870.

The early seventies, the period covered by the sketchbooks, also marked the start of Hannah's and Arthur's career at Doulton & Co. There was an initial period of a few months in 1870 when they were employed, mainly on modelling, on a free-lance basis, followed by a brief spell when Hannah was working at the newly established Minton's Art Pottery Studios at Kensington Gore. This enterprise was another example of the efforts being made to find employment "for such lady students of the Training School as desired it."[16] However, these young assistants simply copied designs supplied by the art director W.S. Colman and others, and were not encouraged to carry out their own ideas. Hannah is remembered by G. Woolliscroft-Rhead as a lady "who had a considerable love for, and facility in drawing animals. Her interest in animals indeed, was the source of much consternation among her feminine fellow-workers; from her habit of bringing mice, frogs, and other livestock to the studio in her pockets."[17] Rhead comments that she "never found the studio an outlet for her artistic energies (and) after a comparatively short period she accepted an appointment at Doulton's, where she found in their grey stoneware a material which was exactly suited to her very individual talent."[18]

Hannah Barlow, now a young lady of twenty years, was already a "character". Her sketchbooks and a scrapbook of individual drawings[19] are filled with humour, much of it of an anthropomorphic kind. "School of Art" dated April 13th 1870 (Figure 12) shows a life class of dog "students" sketching from the live model with a rather severe "art master" dog examining the efforts of a crestfallen pupil. In similar vein an untitled sketch of May 2nd (Figure 13) shows a dog card game, with a cat clawing the back of the seat; there is a pipe-smoking china dog figure on the mantlepiece and a gilt-framed dog portrait on the wall. There is humour also in the trousered duckling, almost Disney-like in its simple cartoon like character (Figure 14).

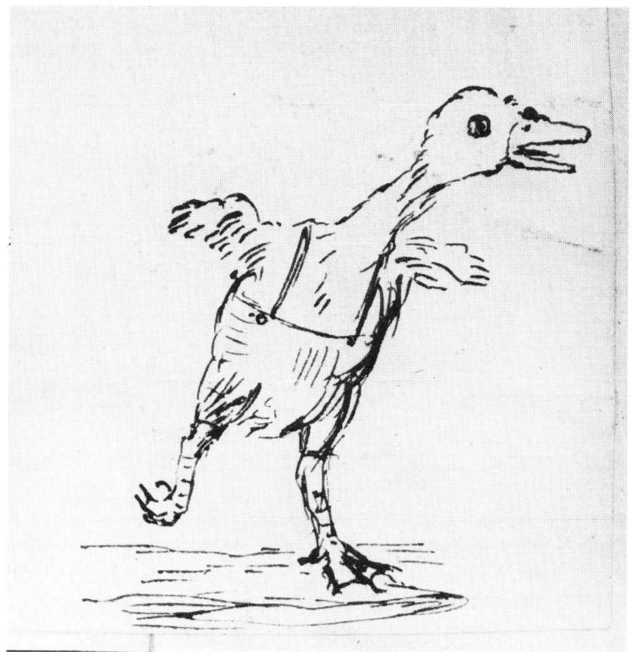

Figure 14: Duck, by Hannah Barlow, c. 1870.

3. DOULTON & CO

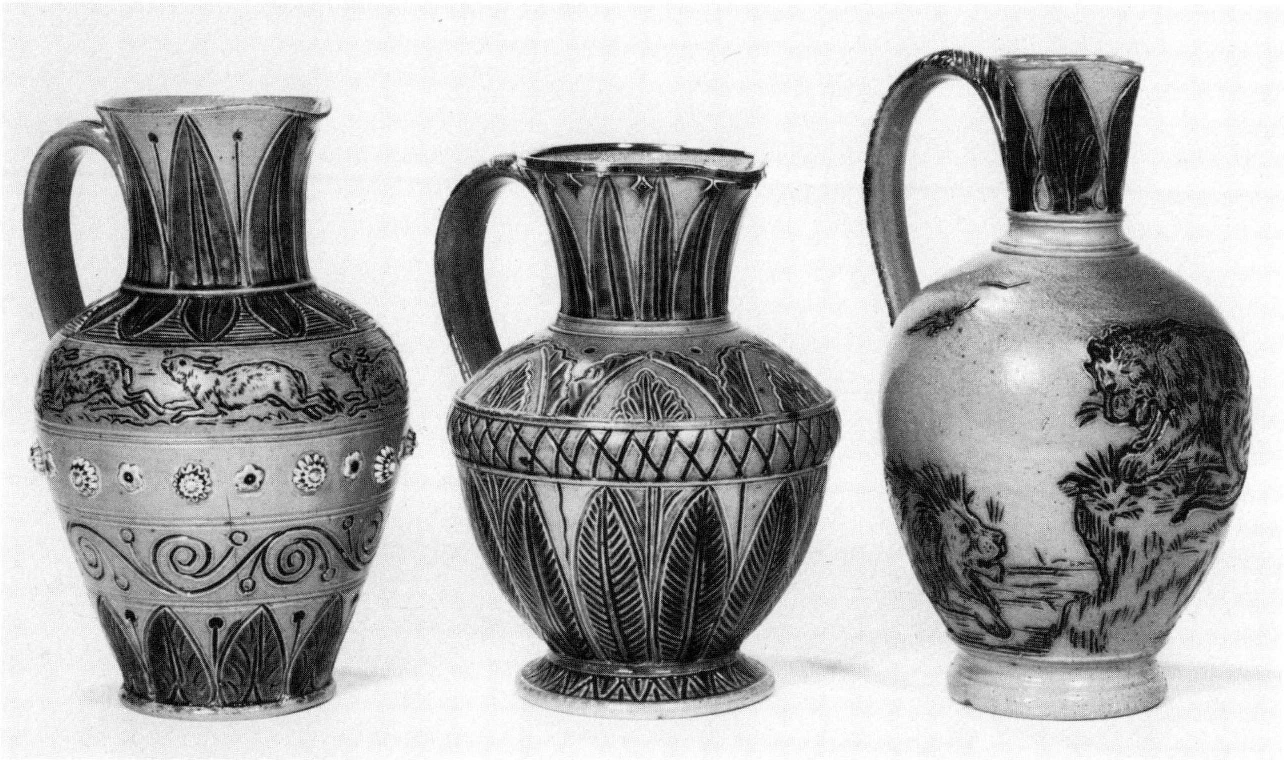

Figure 15: Jug with rabbits, scrolls and stiff leaves, c. 1872, 7½in. Jug with stiff leaves, silver mount, dated 1872, 6¾in. Jug with lions in a landscape, c. 1872, 8in.

From 1871 onwards both Hannah and Arthur were employed by Doulton & Co. on a regular basis. For them both the settled employment was a considerable relief. Hannah wrote later: "When first I came to the Potteries, few people knew what reverses I had had in my home, and what a dreadful undertaking it was to me to meet strangers."[20] They both received almost daily attention from Henry Doulton himself. Edmund Gosse recalls Hannah's account of her first meeting with the great industrialist:

"She was going downstairs early in 1871, and was met by a gentleman tearing up the staircase, two steps at a time, who, nevertheless, paused to take off his hat to her, and to give her a very charming smile. 'I wonder who that is' said Miss Barlow to herself, 'Whoever it is, I feel sure he must be a delightful man to work for.' Very shortly after this, Henry Doulton came to her at her work and introduced himself. In a little while she learned to expect his daily visit, if only for a few moments, always brisk, courteous, enthusiastically encouraging, his suggestions and admiring comments made the work spring up and blossom like a rose."[21]

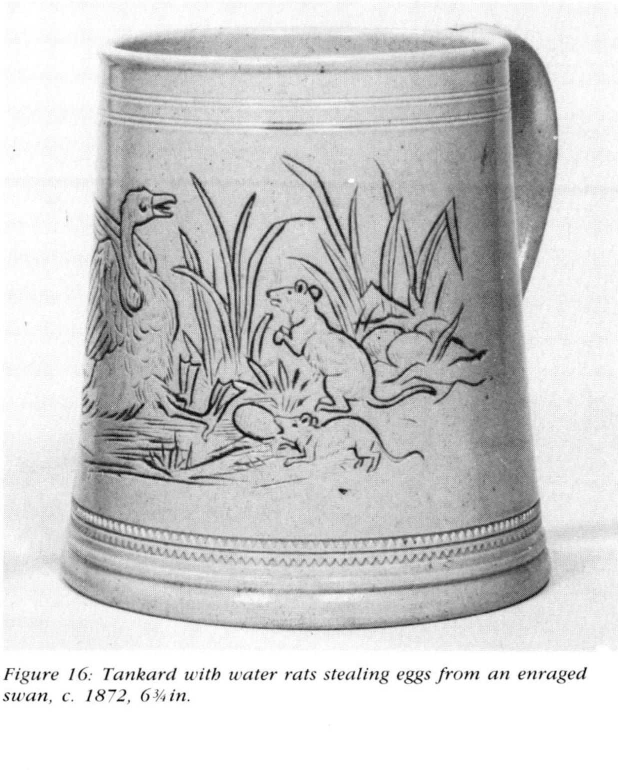

Figure 16: Tankard with water rats stealing eggs from an enraged swan, c. 1872, 6¾in.

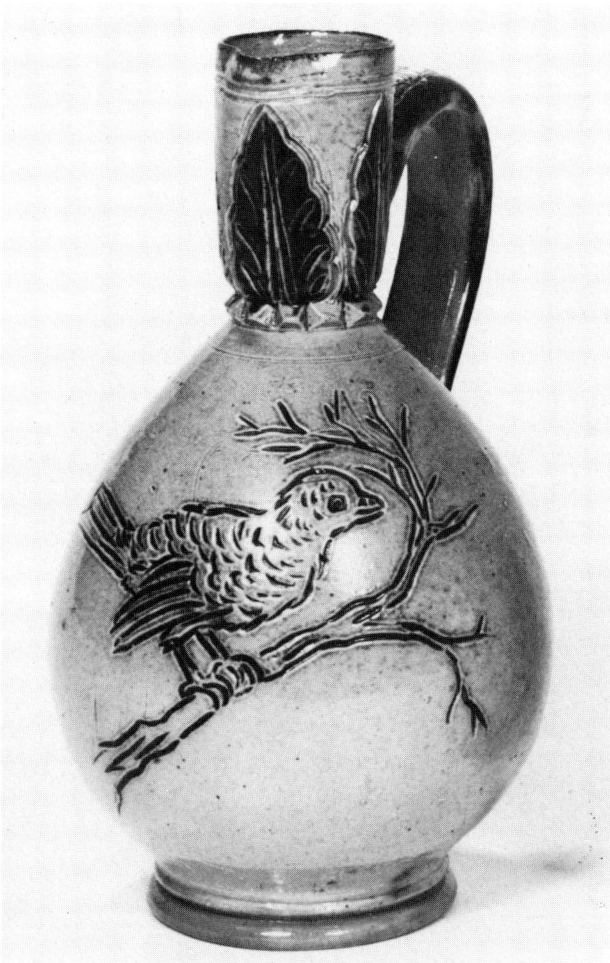

Figure 17: Jug with a garden bird on a branch, c. 1872, 6in.

Henry Doulton's suggestions to her were both specific and helpful: "He would rarely come without telling me of some trait of the life of horses or cattle which he had observed, or some grouping of them in the fields which he believed would aid my imagination."[22] A lightning sketch of horses treading out seed (Figure 19) shows how well Hannah profited from that advice. Despite this immediate sympathy and rapport the arrangements were makeshift initially, for the long term viability of the Art Pottery was still untested. A manuscript recollection of the early days by William Rix,[23] Art Director of the pottery, gives a vivid description of their working conditions at that time:

"They had no studio in which to work. For many months an odd corner of the old showroom . . . was all they had to call their own and customers coming to purchase one or two of the few specimens yet produced persistently intruded on the privacy of the very public studio by craning their necks over the folding screen which indicated the only boundary to the "sanctum" of the Lambeth Art Pottery."[24]

Rix also provides the most detailed account of the development of the pottery leading up to the establishment of the specially built studios in 1873. Progress was signposted by the series of Annual International Exhibitions started in 1871 at the South Kensington Museum. The first of these was held over a period of five months and proved to be a huge popular success, visited by over one million visitors.[25]

Great effort accompanied by much discouraging failure over the previous months had only produced about sixty pieces deemed worthy of sending to the 1871 exhibition. Rix was responsible for delivery and unpacking the pieces. "With a sinking heart the labour and interest of many days were relegated to a dark and shadowy recess under a window-ledge where not one soul in a hundred would ever dream of approaching." However, a guardian angel arrived in the form of Mr

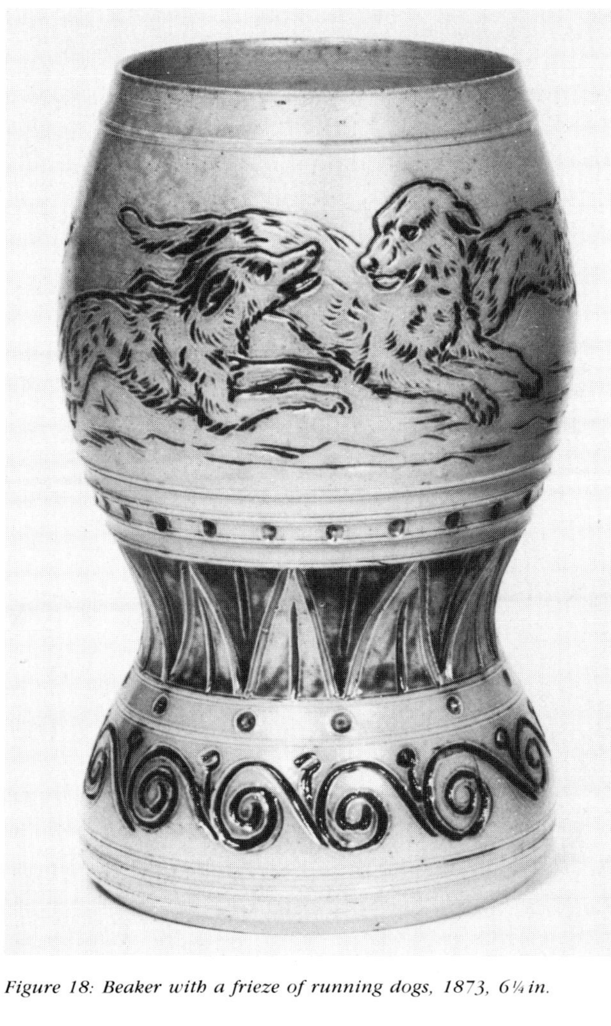

Figure 18: Beaker with a frieze of running dogs, 1873, 6¼in.

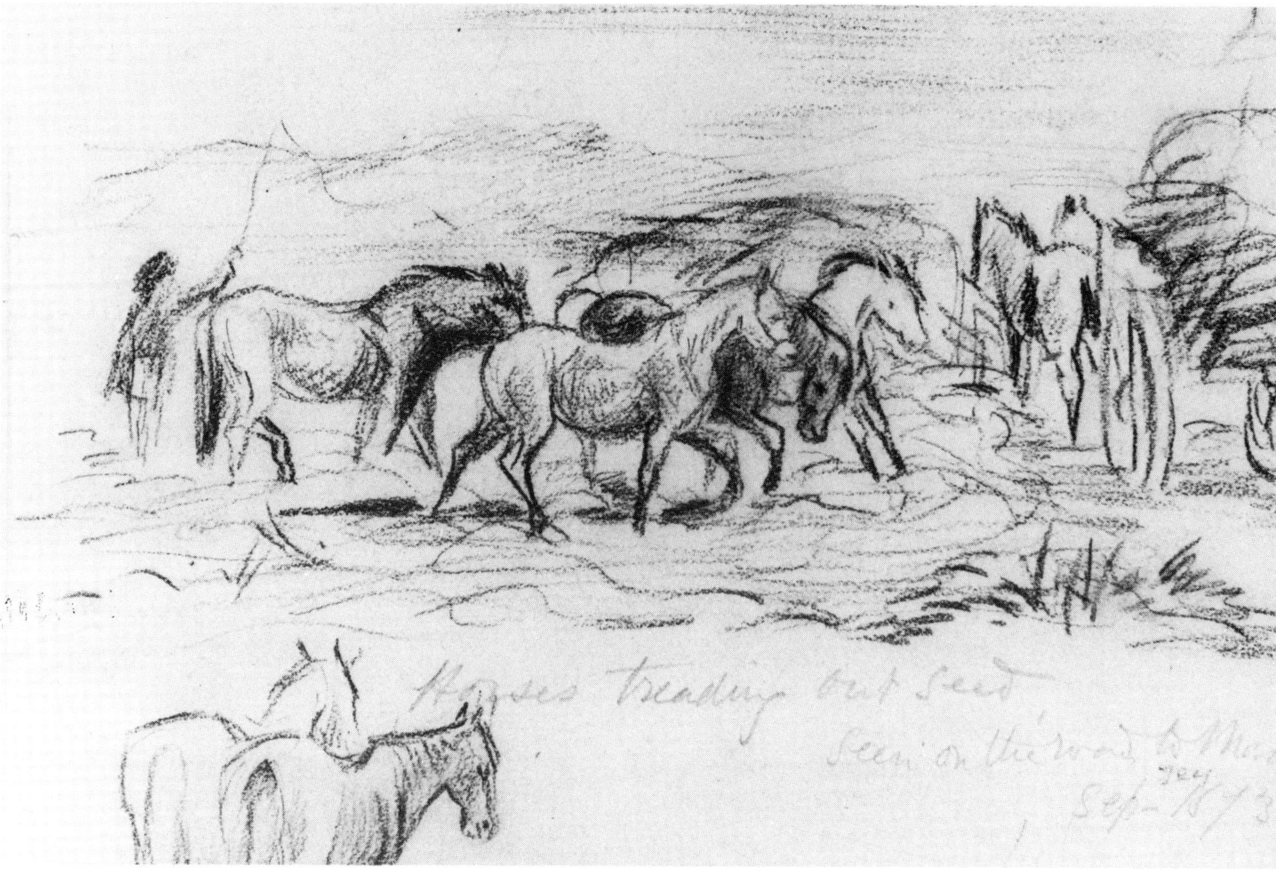

Figure 19: "Horses treading out seed", by Hannah Barlow, 1873.

Soden Smith the exhibition supervisor; he ordered a large glass case to be cleared "and much to the chagrin of other exhibitors, elegant specimens of ceramic work were unceremoniously cast aside to find another lodgment while the 'new stone ware' found itself promoted at one stroke to honour and repute".[26] The display was a huge success and within a few days nearly all the pots were sold to enthusiasts, including foreign museums and Queen Victoria herself.

The extent of Hannah and Arthur's involvement in the 1871 exhibition is unclear. Rix states firmly that it was shortly after the opening of the exhibition that they became involved in the work. Gosse, on the other hand, states that the display included pots and jugs decorated by Tinworth and the Barlows. The Art Journal engravings of the display in the following year (Figures 22 & 23) leave no doubt that, by this time, both of the Barlows were contributors. Surprisingly Rix states that "twelve months of uphill labour seemed to have produced little result and it is certain that at the Exhibition of 1872 the expectation of 1871 were not by any means fulfilled."[27]

The problems were mainly technical and various tools and clay types were experimented with before a satisfactory process of decorating was developed. Initially the inscribing, with an instrument called a "style", was done when the pot was nearly "white hard" but in the spring of 1871 George Tinworth produced the first pieces etched in the soft state. The effect produced was a broader more flowing line which was then filled with blue pigment. Colour was severely restricted and unreliable; the blue frequently turned black in the firing (or disappeared altogether) and the brown turned muddy. Paradoxically the severe technical constraints resulted in purer and more aesthetically pleasing pots than some of the later highly elaborate and technically perfect pieces. Hannah's work is much in evidence in the Art Journal engravings. At this early stage she favoured birds rather than animals, with only a suggestion of background or none at all. She was sometimes content to follow the precedent of Tinworth and her brother, confining herself to their free-flowing foliate designs.

The early restriction to bird and foliate designs was not reflected in the work Hannah was doing in her spare time and in the evenings at Lambeth School of

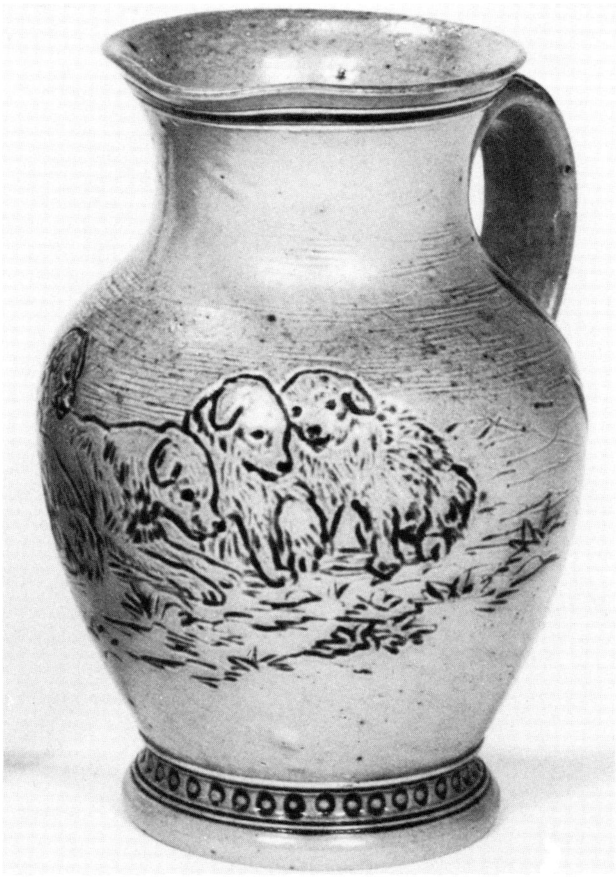

Figure 20: Cream jug with puppies, 1874, 4¾ in.

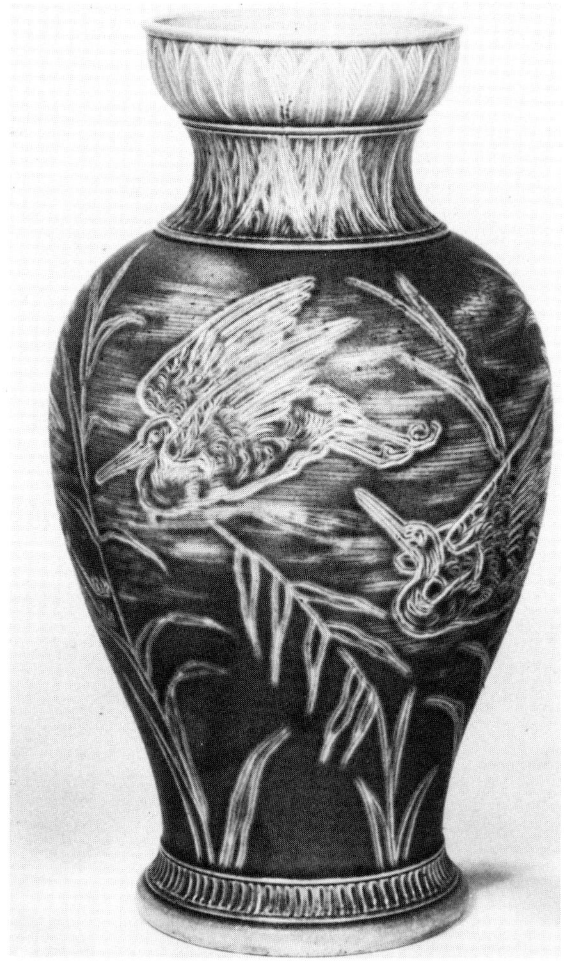

Figure 21: Vase with herons flying amongst reeds, glazed blue on a white ground, 1876, 8¼ in.

Art. She was in a fever of creative activity exploring and evolving the major features of the repertory of ideas which would serve her for the rest of her career. The set half-hour timed sketches developed her facility for achieving effects directly and rapidly. A large number of these survive in her scrapbook revealing how she managed to turn the set subjects towards one or other of her favourite themes. "Defiance: Butcher coming for her lamb" (Figure 25) shows her concern for protecting the weak. Children are frequently the virtuous guardians but more characteristically animals defend their own kind or, in unlikely amity with other species, fend off attack by man or beast. In one drawing a dog defends a horse against his cruel master; in another, a finely detailed pen drawing dated January 1870 entitled "Retribution" (figure 26), pigs protect their young from a marauding wild dog. A drawing dated 28 October 1870 (Figure 27) portrays wild dogs attacking sheep with the distant farmer apparently ignoring the carnage.

A number of very competent and fluent drawings of this period are annoted "Drawn by left hand" indicating that Hannah was ambidextrous. The later account[28] which appeared in the Berlin "National Zeitung" in 1876 about her losing the use of her right hand through constant contact with damp clay is therefore perhaps romanticising when it suggests that it took her many weeks of practice to develop the use of her left hand.

Other set subjects pasted into the scrapbook have a pottery design bias: decorative handles for vases (Figures 28, 29 & 30) employing a naturalistic style reminiscent of the then fashionable majolica ware; oval relief modelled mirror frames (Figure 31) using goats, sheep and even frogs as decorative motifs formed into ingenious flowing borders. None of these designs however appear to have been put into production, although occasionally pots incorporate animals modelled in relief. Hannah explored the possibility of tile designing, making up sets of tiles for fireplace surrounds, panels for furniture or similar purposes. "Ye Seven Ages of Ye Dog" provides a

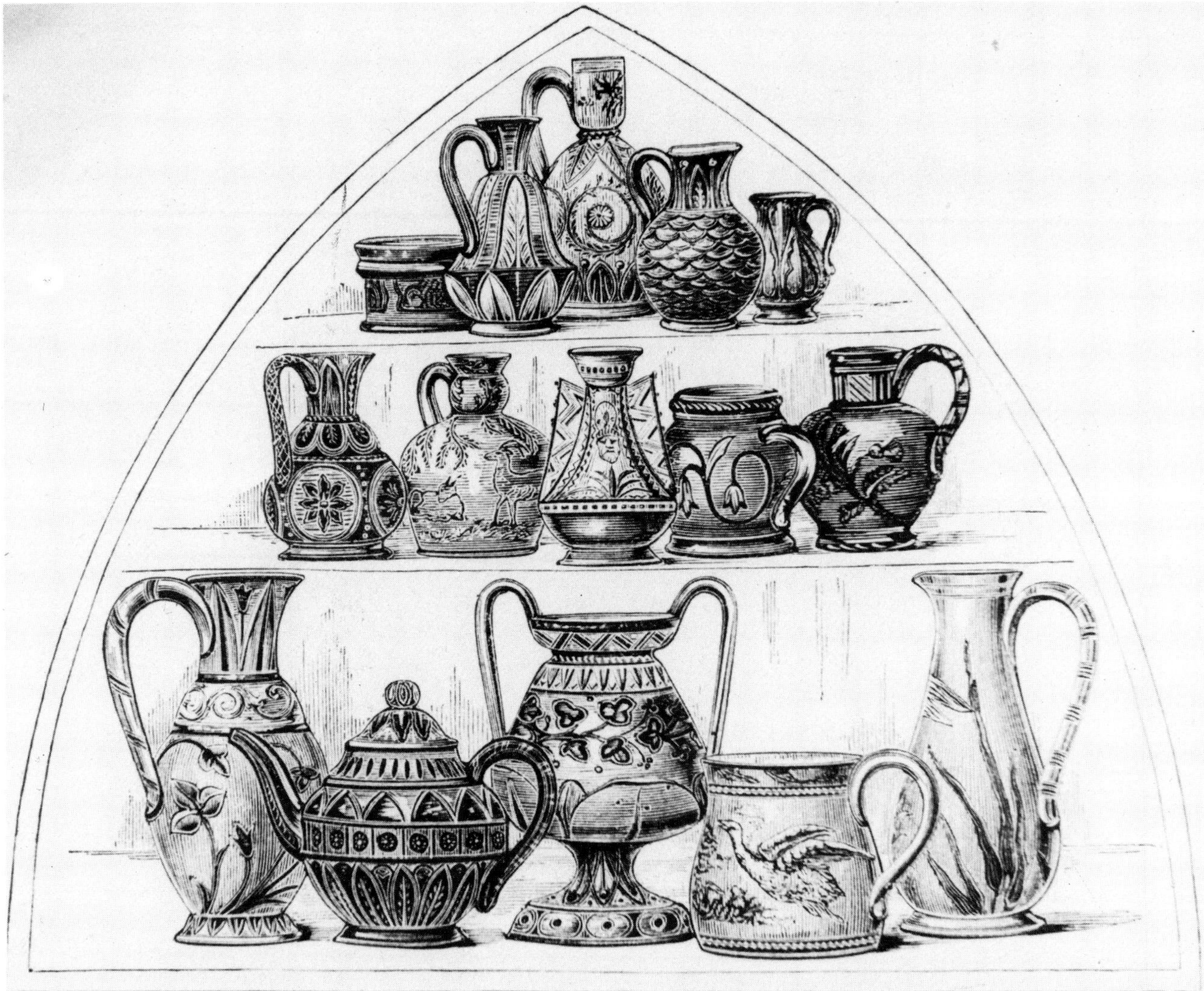

Figure 22: Annual International Exhibition, South Kensington, 1872.

canine equivalent to the Seven Ages of Man, a popular subject explored by others, including Stacy Marks for Minton's Art Pottery at Kensington Gore. The second stage "Childhood" shows a young puppy with tail between its legs watched over by its parent (Figure 32). An ebonised sideboard designed by Charles Bevan for Gillow & Co. incorporates tiles carried out by Hannah Barlow: it was purchased from the 1872 Annual International Exhibition by the South Kensington Museum (Figure 33). Perhaps the most bizarre exercise of all was designing a set of rustic letters incorporating insects and other crawling creatures, forming the initials of H.B.B. (Figure 24).

Although many of the drawings, sketches and designs in the scrapbook bear a close relationship to later work carried out in the pottery studios there does not appear to have been any direct copying from this source. Contemporary accounts of Hannah's method of work lay stress on the immediate, seemingly spontaneous nature of her inspiration. The absence of copies derived from such a comprehensive collection as the scrapbook strongly supports that view.

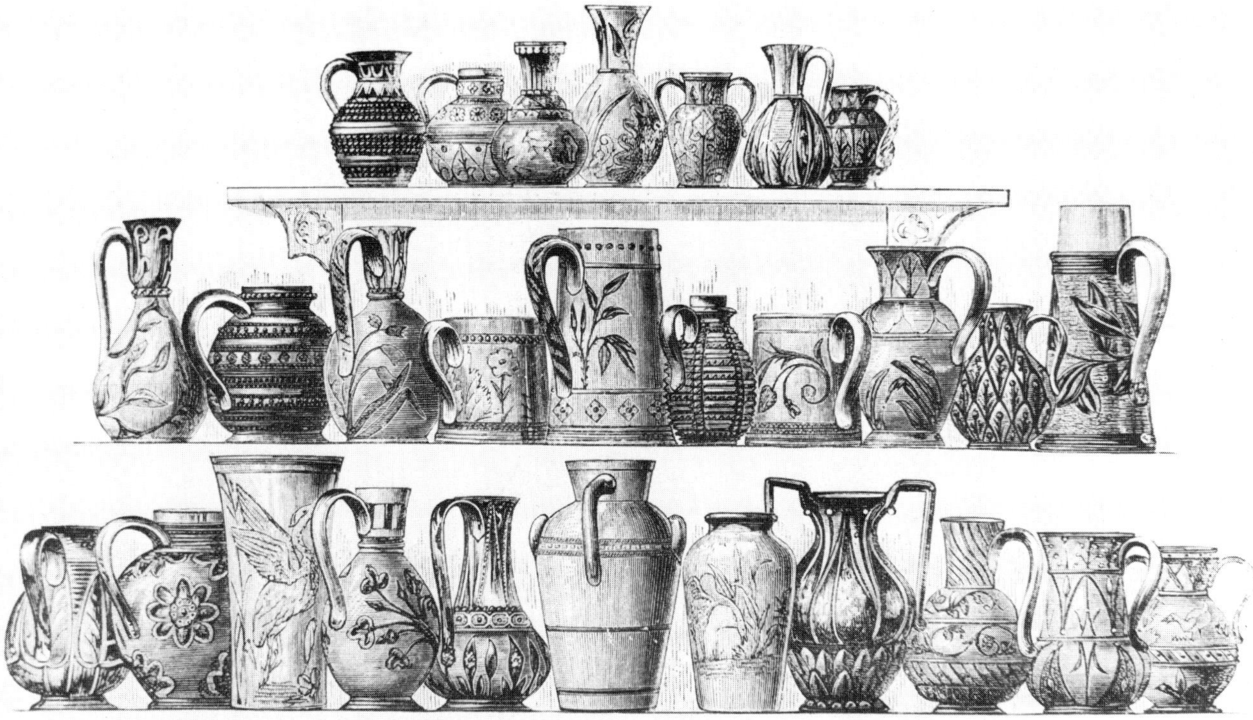

Figure 23: Annual International Exhibition, South Kensington, 1872.

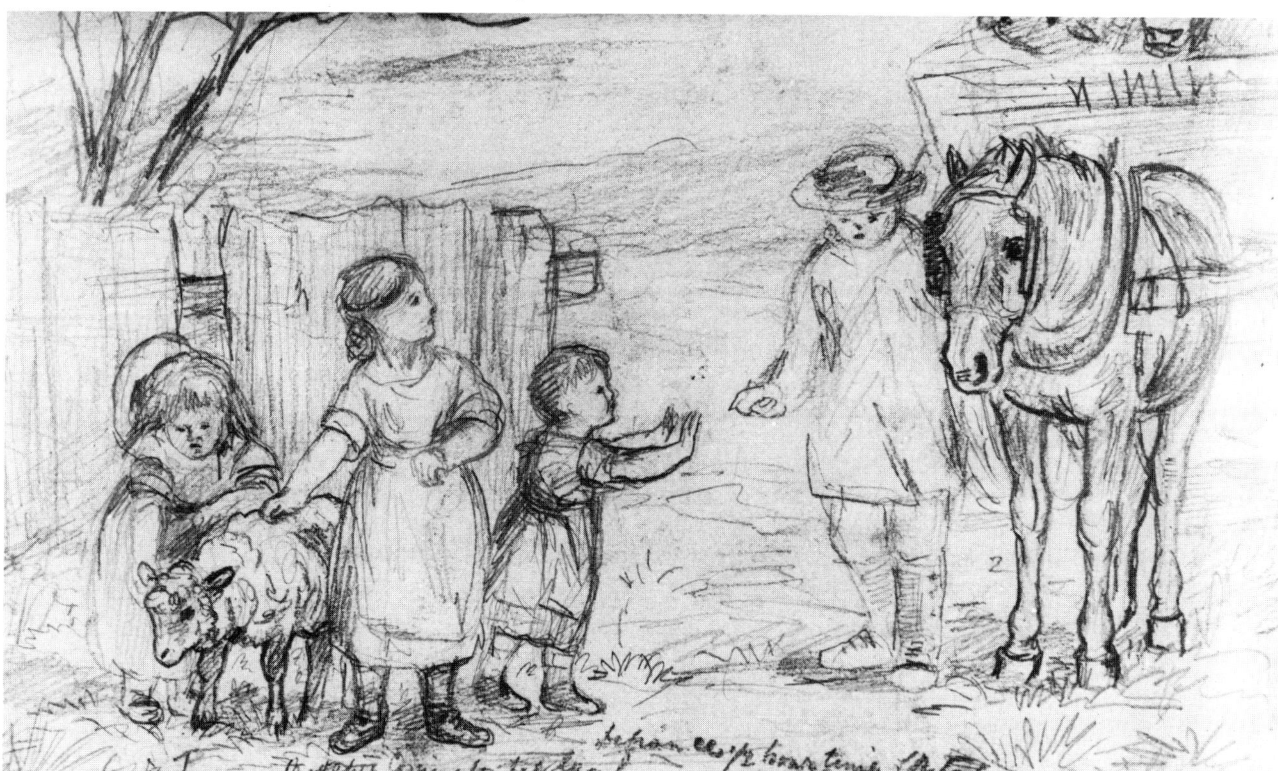

Figure 25: "Defiance: Butcher coming for her lamb", half hour time sketch by Hannah Barlow, c. 1870.

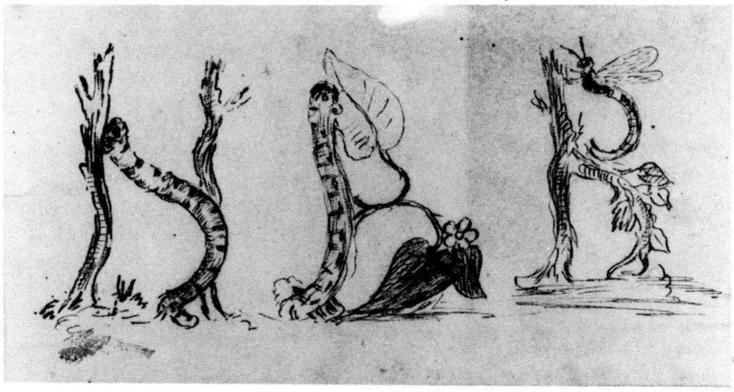

Figure 24: The initials H.B.B. in "insect" lettering, Hannah Barlow, c. 1870.

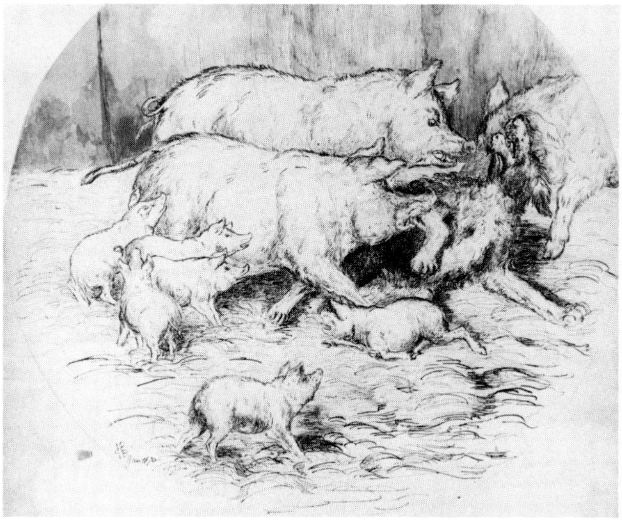

Figure 26: "Retribution", by Hannah Barlow, 1870.

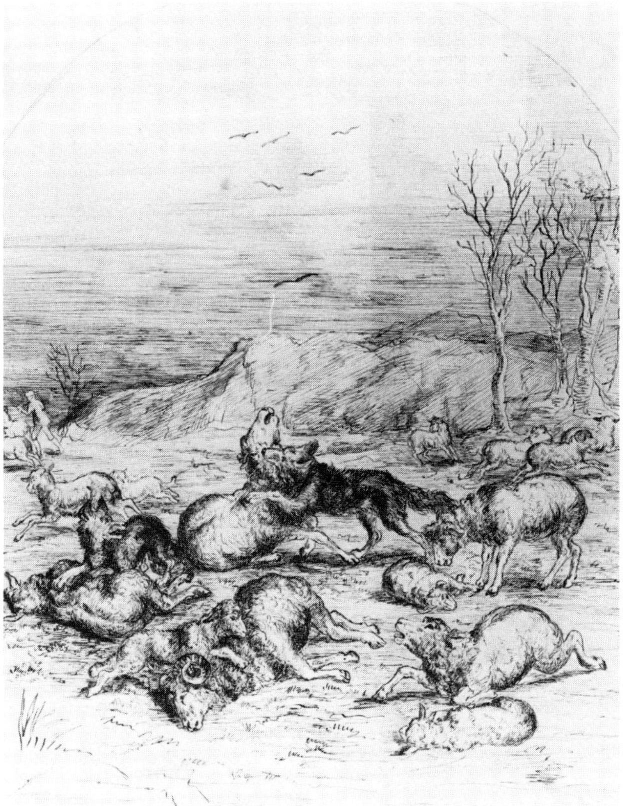

Figure 27: Wild dogs attacking sheep, by Hannah Barlow, c. 1870.

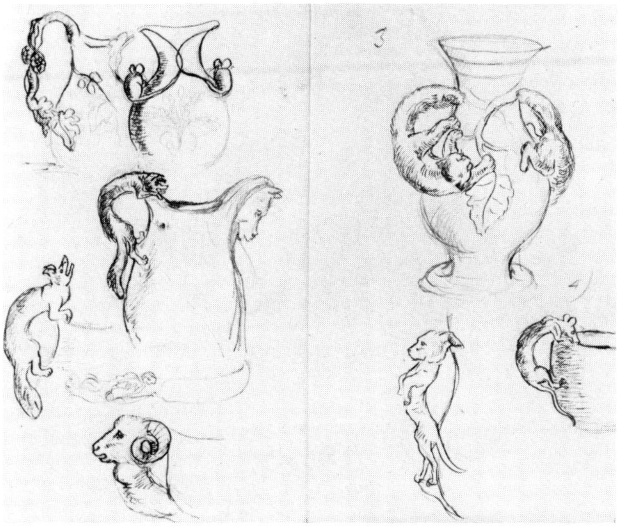

Figure 28: Designs for decorative handles, by Hannah Barlow, c. 1870.

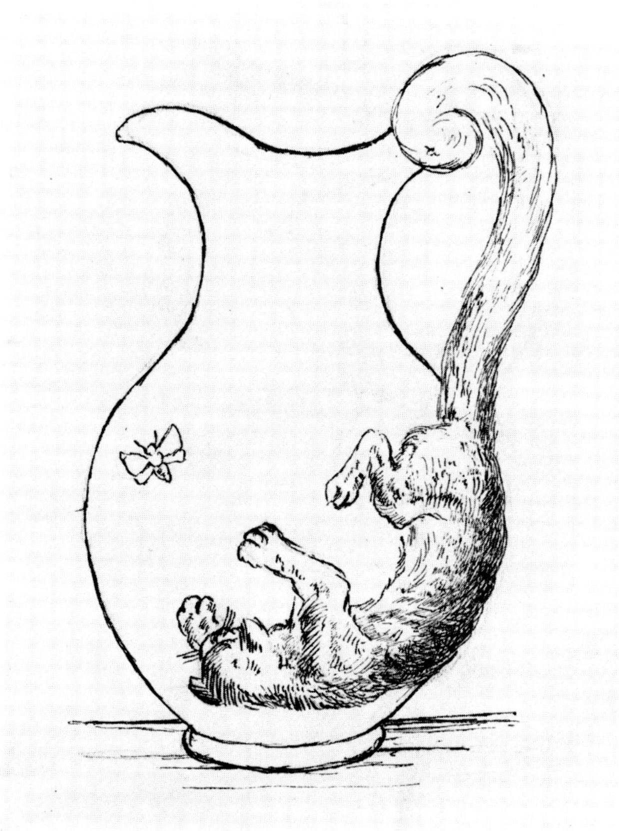

Figure 29: Design for "Cat" jug handle, by Hannah Barlow, c. 1870.

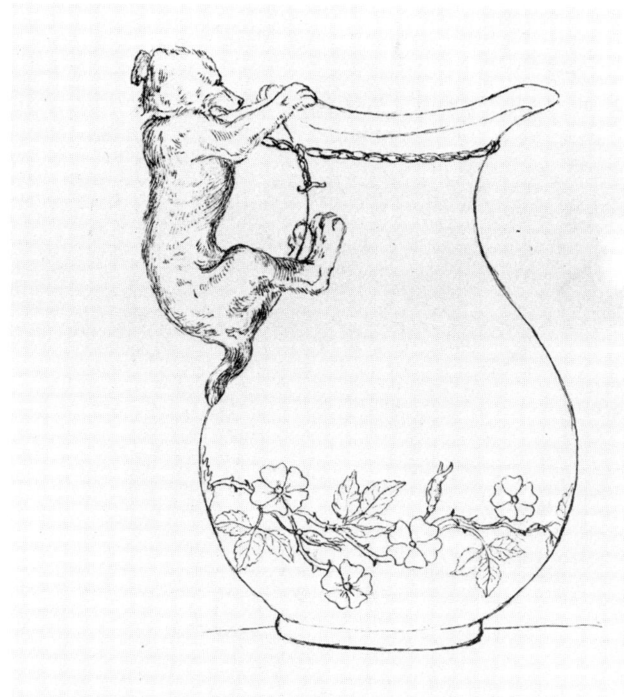

Figure 30: Design for "Dog" jug handle, by Hannah Barlow, c. 1870.

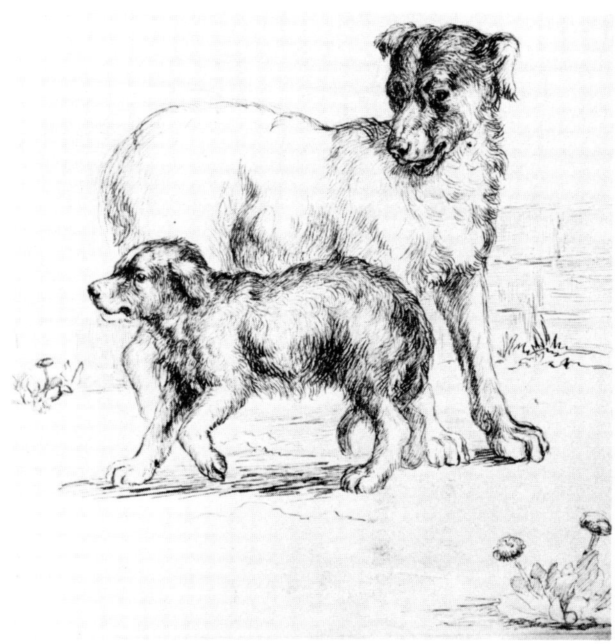

Figure 32: "Ye Seven Ages of Ye Dog" by Hannah Barlow, c. 1870.

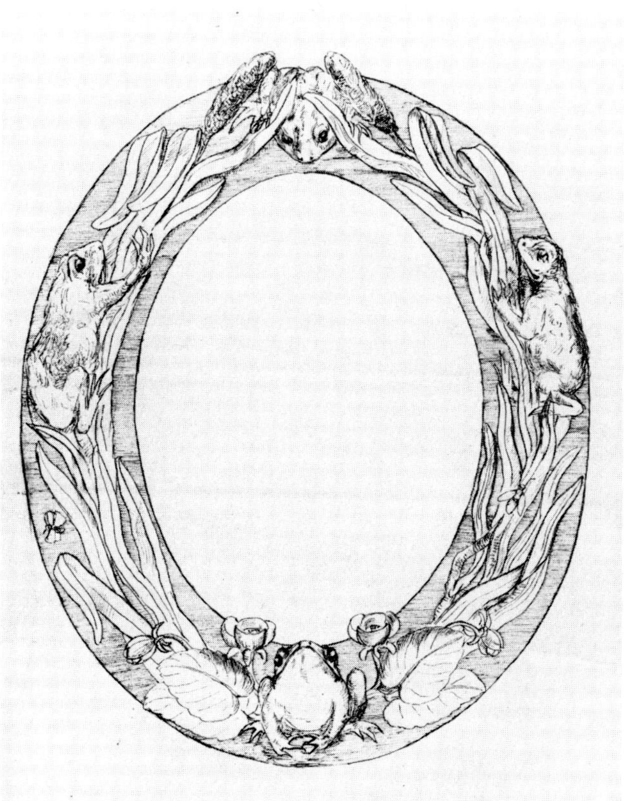

Figure 31: Design for "Frog" mirror frame by Hannah Barlow, c. 1870.

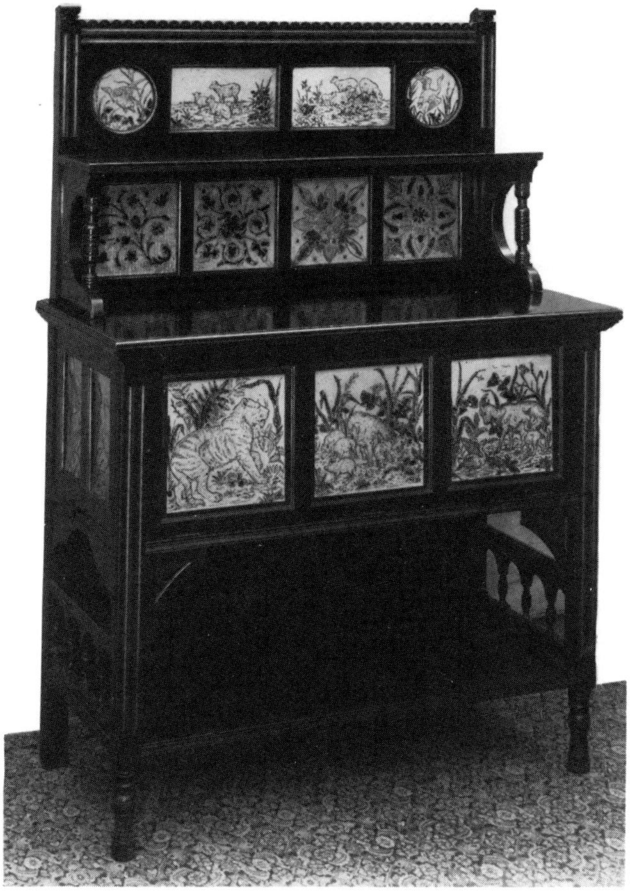

Figure 33: Sideboard designed by Charles Bevan for Gillow & Co. Panels by Hannah Barlow, 1872.

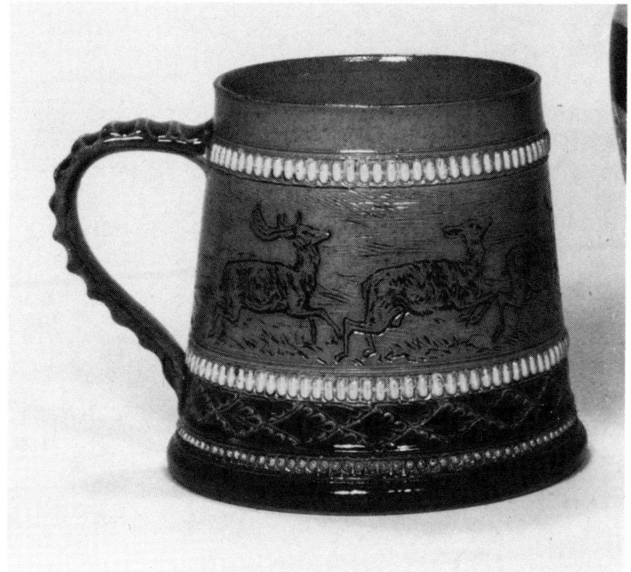

Figure 34: Mug with a frieze of deer, 1875, 3½ in.

4. THE ART STUDIOS

The two years of development following the start of Hannah and Arthur's regular employment at Doulton & Co. culminated in the creation of special studios for the growing band of pottery decorators. John Sparkes again played a crucial role in urging Henry Doulton forward. Gosse gives an account of a conversation between the two friends in a hansom cab, returning to Lambeth after visiting an exhibition of Art Pottery in a fashionable West-End shop. It was "thin, washy stuff" according to Henry Doulton and then "after a moment's pause, with his great eyes, brimful of eagerness, fixed upon Mr Sparkes, 'Can't we make Lambeth the centre of a real art product? Don't you think we could work the matter out systematically and really do it properly? Have you the students? Can you send me a whole batch of them?'"[29]

The answer to all these questions fired at Sparkes was of course an enthusiastically affirmative one. Work soon began on converting the many small rooms in a block of workmen's houses (which had ceased to be used) into ranges of studios. The adaptations were completed early in 1873 and "Mr Sparkes, on a wet and dismal day . . . started from the Art School with a procession of students, male and female, all of whom were duly given more or less permanent engagements, and distributed throughout the little houses prepared for them."[30] Included in that marching band were several destined to take a leading role as decorators in the firm: Bessie Youatt, Emily Edwards, Elizabeth Fisher, Eliza Simmance, Eliza Banks, the deaf and dumb Frank Butler, and perhaps, most importantly for Hannah and Arthur, their younger sister Florence.

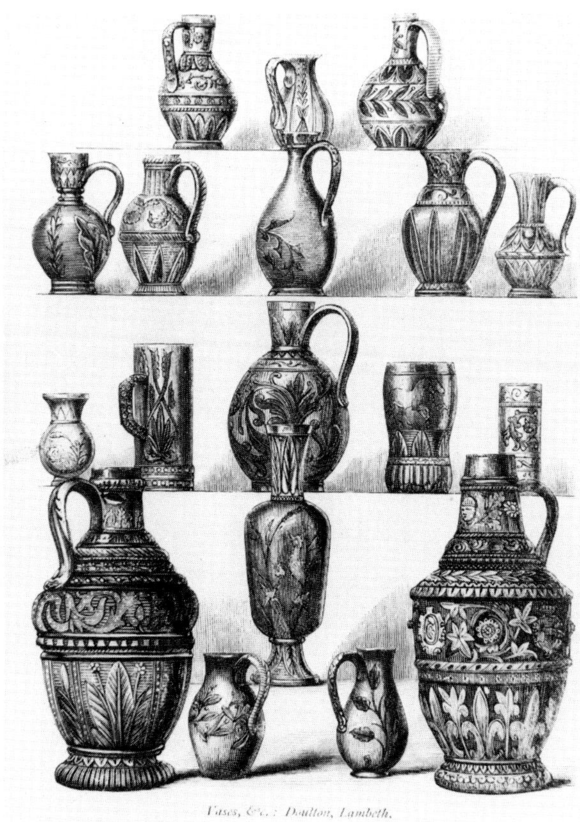

Figure 35: The Universal Exhibition, Vienna, 1873.

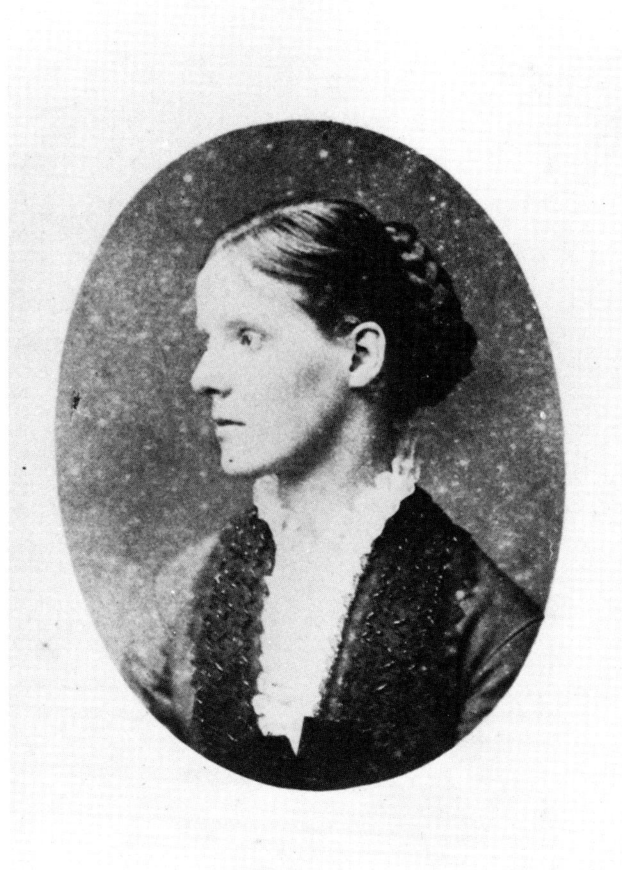

Figure 36: Florence Elizabeth Barlow, c. 1877.

Expansion of the studios meant that other types of Art Pottery could be developed alongside the salt-glaze ware. Faience was the first of these, although output initially was very limited and Rix records only thirty or forty pieces a week being made. However the technical problems, which reduced the output of successful pieces still further, were solved in time to include pieces in the 1873 Vienna Universal

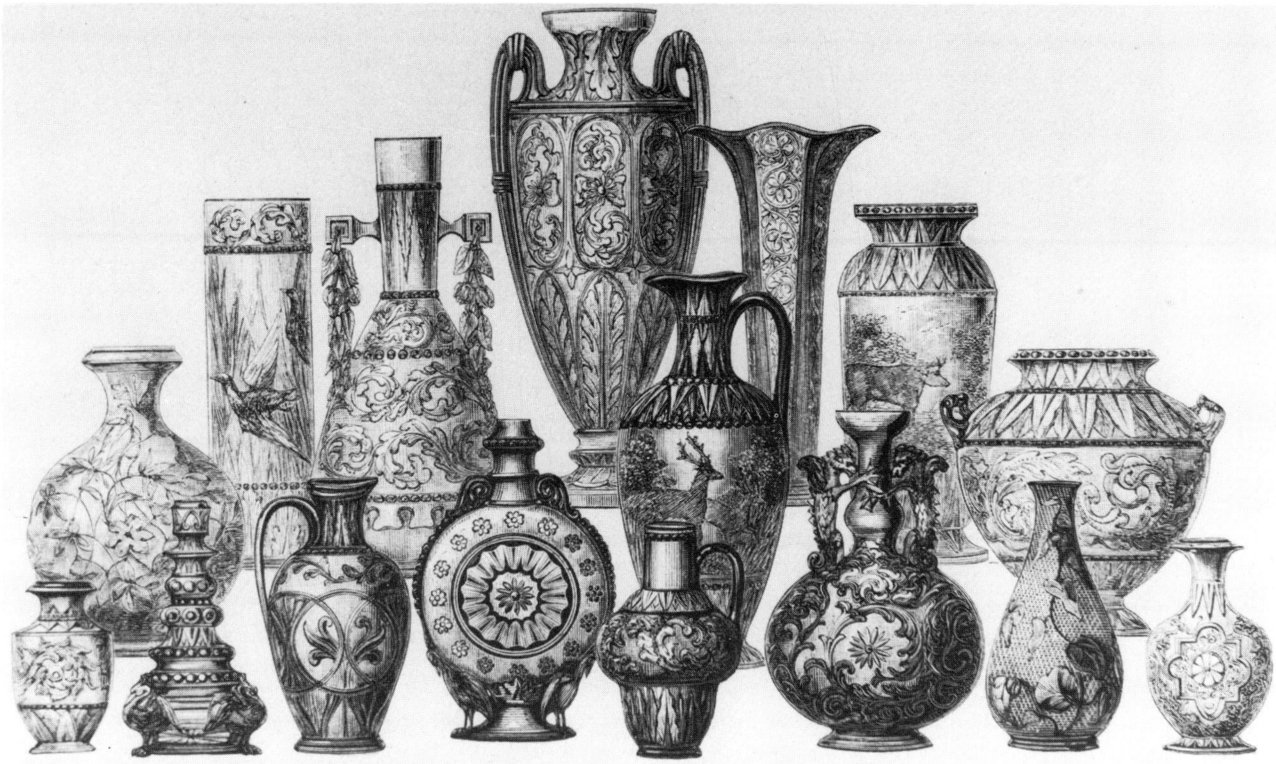

Figure 37: The Paris International Exhibition, 1878.

Exhibition. The Art Journal illustrates a group of exhibits but these are all salt-glaze ware (Figure 35); indeed all the artists identified in that inaugural procession worked in salt-glaze techniques rather than faience. Much later on Hannah and Florence occasionally worked in that essentially painterly method of decoration but at this time like Arthur they were working exclusively on stoneware. The Art Journal illustration shows two vases almost certainly by Hannah, one with birds and another with a frieze of horses: the two massively large jugs are in the style of Arthur Barlow showing his use of sculptural carving, a technique which he favoured.

The enlargement of the Art Studios created the need for changes of practice which had major and to some extent unforeseen consequences. Each studio contained several workers organised in a hierarchy: at the head was the artist decorator who was in charge of a senior and perhaps several junior assistants. This arrangement ensured that much of the routine detail, beading, painting and such like, was delegated by the head of the studio. Increasingly artist decorators would share responsibility for a vase (or most likely a pair) with one creating the surrounding or border pattern and the other, probably more senior artist, working on a blank panel or frieze. This develoment took several years to evolve and it was not until the eighties that Hannah generally adopted the practice of confining her own work to a reserve area or an already partly decorated piece. Hannah and Florence worked together and, for much of the time, shared a large studio between them; they frequently co-operated on the decoration of a vase or jug, initially with Florence as assistant but later on an equal basis. Their styles were virtually identical until the late seventies, although Florence's strong pattern sense survived long after Hannah had lost interest in formalised decoration. Vases decorated by Florence in the early years can be easily confused with the work of Hannah; she became adept at drawing horses, birds and other creatures in a close pastiche of her sister's style. The introduction of the pâte-sur-pâte technique first shown at the Paris International Exhibition of 1878 (Figure 37) allowed Florence to develop a distinctive style, for Hannah seldom used the technique. At this time an informal agreement between the sisters divided the animal and bird kingdoms so that Florence's work from then onwards is confined to birds treated naturalistically using the new technique: at a much later period the birds are sometimes drawn in a highly formalised manner with strong overtones of Art-Nouveau.

Other changes following the expansion of the studio included a system of dating and a method of identifying individual pots for stock record purposes. Dating was introduced in 1873 and discontinued in the mid-eighties: it was re-introduced in 1902 in a coded form. The decision to abandon such a seemingly useful device was in response to complaints from retailers that they could not sell vases which, through the date visible on the base, customers could easily identify as old stock. Each artist evolved a distinctive monogram or mark which was almost invariably inscribed or pressed onto the base (the exception was Tinworth who inscribed his mark on the side). A sequence of numbers was added to the monograms of major artists; these ran consecutively following a yearly cycle. These more sophisticated methods of identification became necessary because of the sheer volume of production, running into several thousand pieces each year. It seems likely that for at least a twenty year period both Hannah and Florence were producing three or four pots per working day, averaging about a thousand pieces each over a year.

Early in 1876 Arthur's health suddenly deteriorated. For the past six years he had managed to drag himself about on crutches, helped on and off omnibuses by his sister, a compassionate conductor, or passengers. In wet weather he was unable to protect himself and in consequence developed rheumatism: he frequently stumbled and fell causing further damage to his twisted body. Despite dreadful suffering and frequent illness he attended evening classes at the Royal Academy Schools from the start of 1872 and continued to work at Lambeth School of Art under Sparkes throughout the period. In the spring of 1876

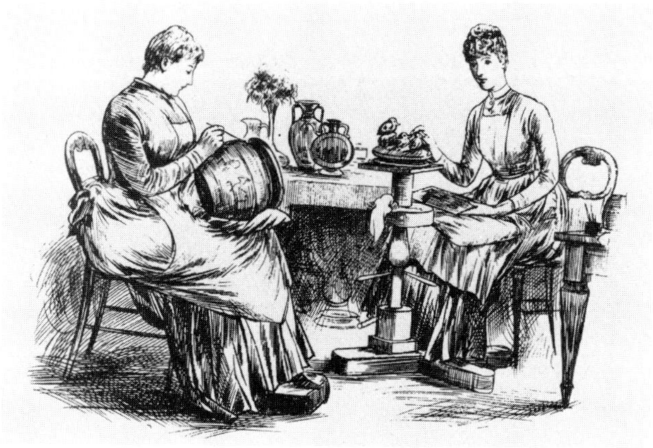

Figure 38: Hannah and Florence Barlow in their studio; The Lady, 1887.

it became no longer possible for Arthur to continue working and, after devoted nursing by his mother, he was taken home to Bishop's Stortford. Later in the summer he was well enough to be taken to Derbyshire accompanied for part of the time by his sister Hannah. A disease of the kidneys was diagnosed and it became clear that no full recovery could be expected. He remained at home until, in the following year, Mrs Barlow decided to move her remaining family to London. In August 1877 all the unmarried members of the family, including Hannah and Florence, were re-united under one roof. The house was No 55, Loughborough Park, Brixton (then considered to be a sheltered and healthy locality) and possessing a large

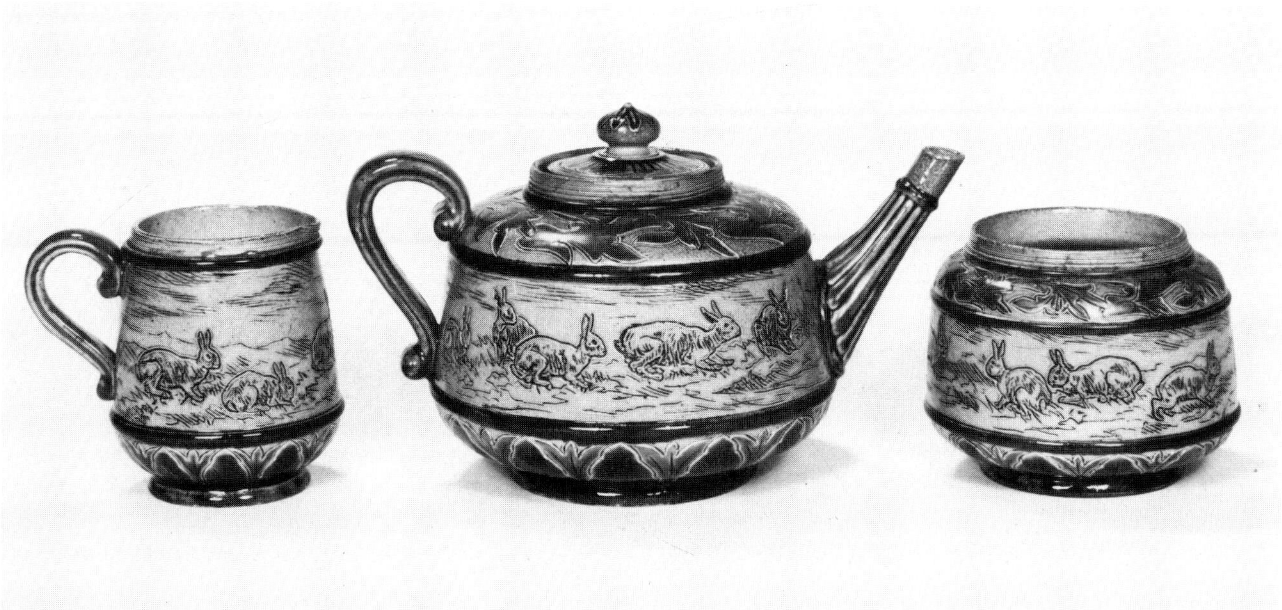

Figure 39: Teaset with rabbits, borders by Lucy Barlow, 1883, teapot 4½ in.

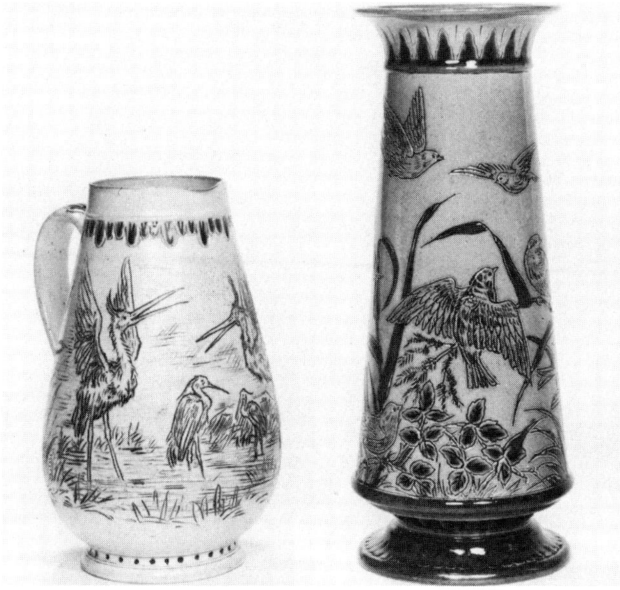

Figure 40: Jug by Florence Barlow with herons, 1874, 7½ in. Vase by Florence Barlow with finches, 1878, 11in.

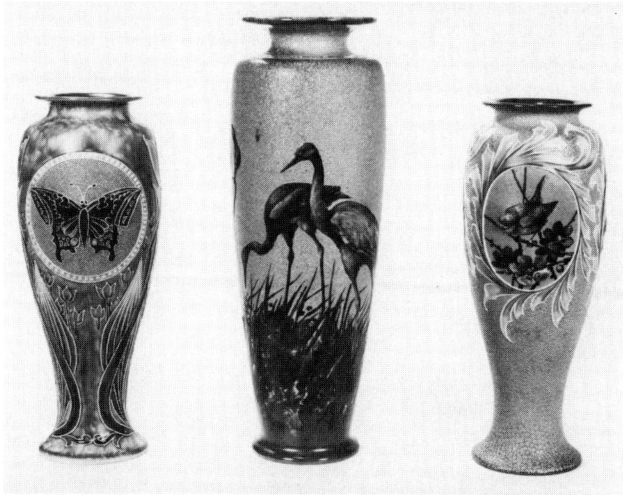

Figure 41: Vases by Florence Barlow, piped butterfly and tulips, c. 1906, 11¾ in. Pâte-sur-pâte storks, 1906, 14¼ in. Three panels of garden birds with borders by Frank Butler, 1903, 11½ in.

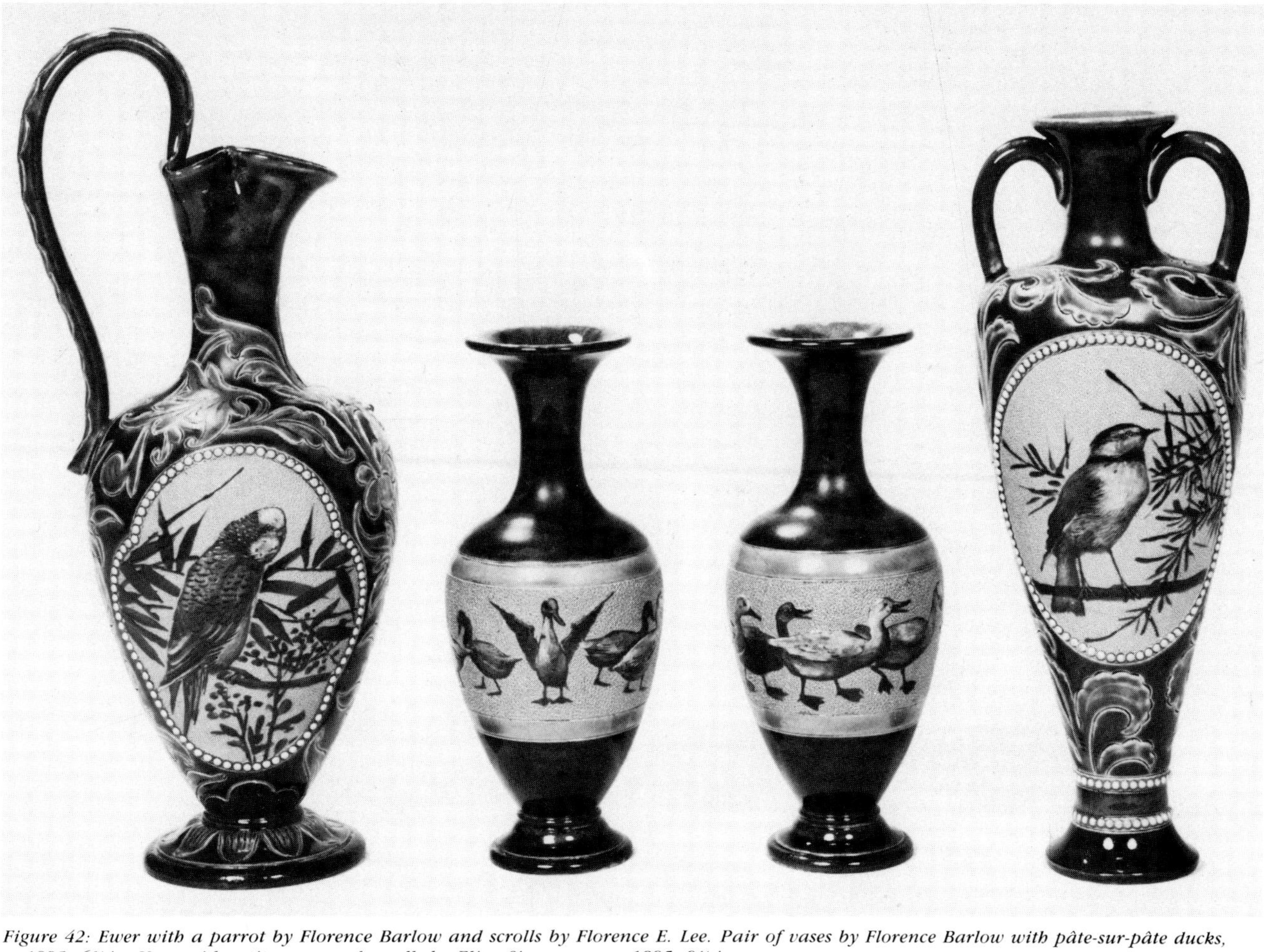

Figure 42: Ewer with a parrot by Florence Barlow and scrolls by Florence E. Lee. Pair of vases by Florence Barlow with pâte-sur-pâte ducks, c. 1895, 6¾ in. Vase with a titmouse and scrolls by Eliza Simmance, c. 1895, 9½ in.

garden. Arthur remained confined to bed except for short periods, when he would visit the seaside looked after by Hannah, Florence and his younger brother Hubert. In early February 1879 he died.

1876, the year of Arthur's relapse, ironically for the grieving Barlow family, was a period of triumphant achievement for the Art Pottery Studios. A large collection of nearly a thousand pieces had been assembled for the Philadelphia International Exhibition, consisting of both salt-glaze and faience. Before shipping the collection to America it was decided to stage an exhibition of the pieces in the showrooms at Lambeth. The show was a tremendous success with over 1,500 visitors in three days including

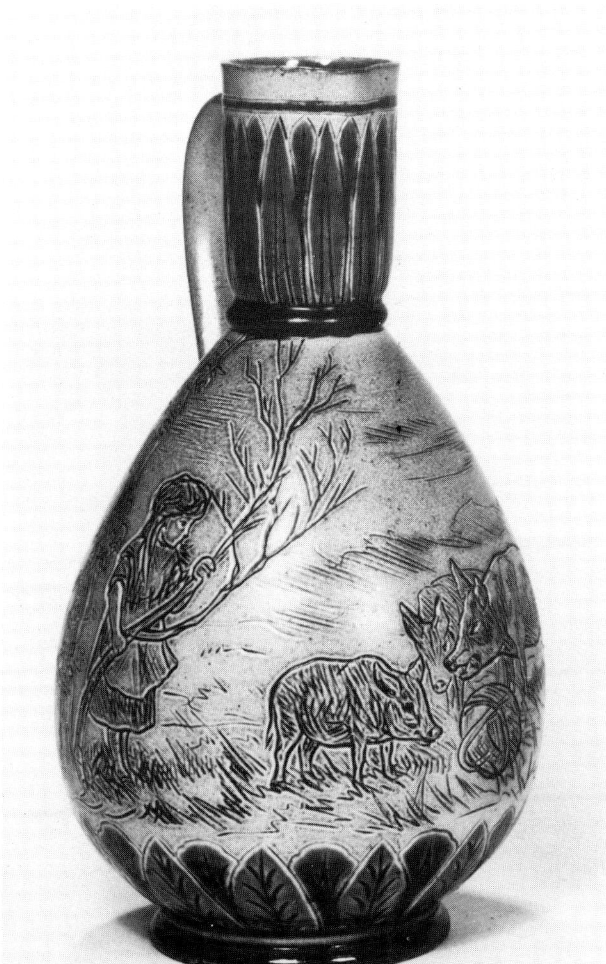

Figure 43: Jug with a young girl watching pigs surrounding her upturned basket, borders by Lucy Barlow, 1883, 8¾in.

John Ruskin and the great Liberal statesman William Ewart Gladstone, then in his late sixties, no longer Prime Minister but still an awe-inspiring public figure.

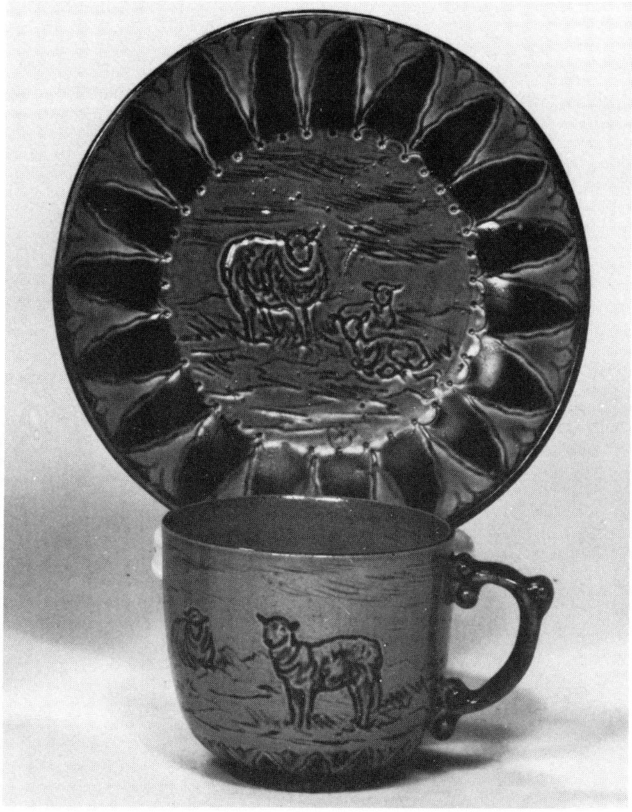

Figure 44: Cup and saucer with sheep and lambs, borders by Rosina Brown, 1884, cup 2in.

The Art Journal in reviewing the Philadelphia exhibition referred to the Lambeth pottery as "not only . . . known and estimated in every town of these Kingdoms but throughout Europe; and now they will obtain renown in the New World."[31]

Later in the same year the Art Journal reported a presentation by students and ex-students to John Sparkes at the annual prize giving at Lambeth School of Art. Sparkes had been appointed head master of the Government School of Design, South Kensington and it was therefore assumed that he would be ceasing all connection with Lambeth. The concept of a full time professional post excluding other work had not yet evolved and it was possible to hold two or more appointments simultaneously. Consequently Sparkes retained the directorship of Lambeth in addition to the new post. The good news had the effect of redoubling the efforts of the students to make the presentation a worthy one, for they saw it as an opportunity to express gratitude to their hero who had done so much for vocational art education, and was not, after all, deserting them.

The gratitude of the women employed at the Lambeth studios for the opportunities offered them by Henry Doulton was shown some years later in a particularly striking form. An illuminated address was presented to mark the tenth anniversary of the introduction of women into the Art Pottery: "The undersigned being the whole of the Lady Artists and Assistants now engaged in the studios upon the work desire to take this opportunity of expressing our obligations to you for the origination of an occupation at once interesting and elevating to so large a number of our sex. We also desire to record our very high appreciation of the arrangements made for our comfort and convenience in the various sections."[32] Vignettes in the borders of the illuminated address show idyllic scenes of women potters in Greek costume, arrangements of pots, and one group entirely devoted to the work of Hannah Barlow — whose personal anniversary it was. Over 200 women's names are included in the presentation and a short supplement listed the men also.

Despite the competition Hannah remained the most highly regarded and widely known of the women artist decorators. Gosse recalls that during one of John Ruskin's visits to the pottery Henry Doulton "asked him to accept whichever piece of Doulton ware had pleased him most, the great critic, after much reflection, said 'I will have, please, the jug, with all the little piggies scurrying round under the handle'. This, it is almost needless to say, was one of Miss Hannah Barlow's animal pieces."[33]

5. A SETTLED CAREER

After the rapid expansion of the studios in the seventies, the eighties was a period of relative stability for the Art Pottery. The market for the traditional salt-glaze and faience had become saturated and new lines were introduced to stimulate public interest. In reviews of the regular exhibition of new stock held in the Doulton showrooms, by the editor of Studio Notes, Walter Gandy and others, there are recurring references to "the present excessive stagnation of trade (causing) the sales to be very small".[34] Although no blame is directed at the artistic merits of the ware produced, detailed criticism is made of extravagant use of decoration, excessive use of gold, slowness in the work of assistants, resulting in uneconomically high prices. Undoubtedly prices were substantial, a pair of pots could be retailed at more than the weekly wage of a Senior Assistant.[35]

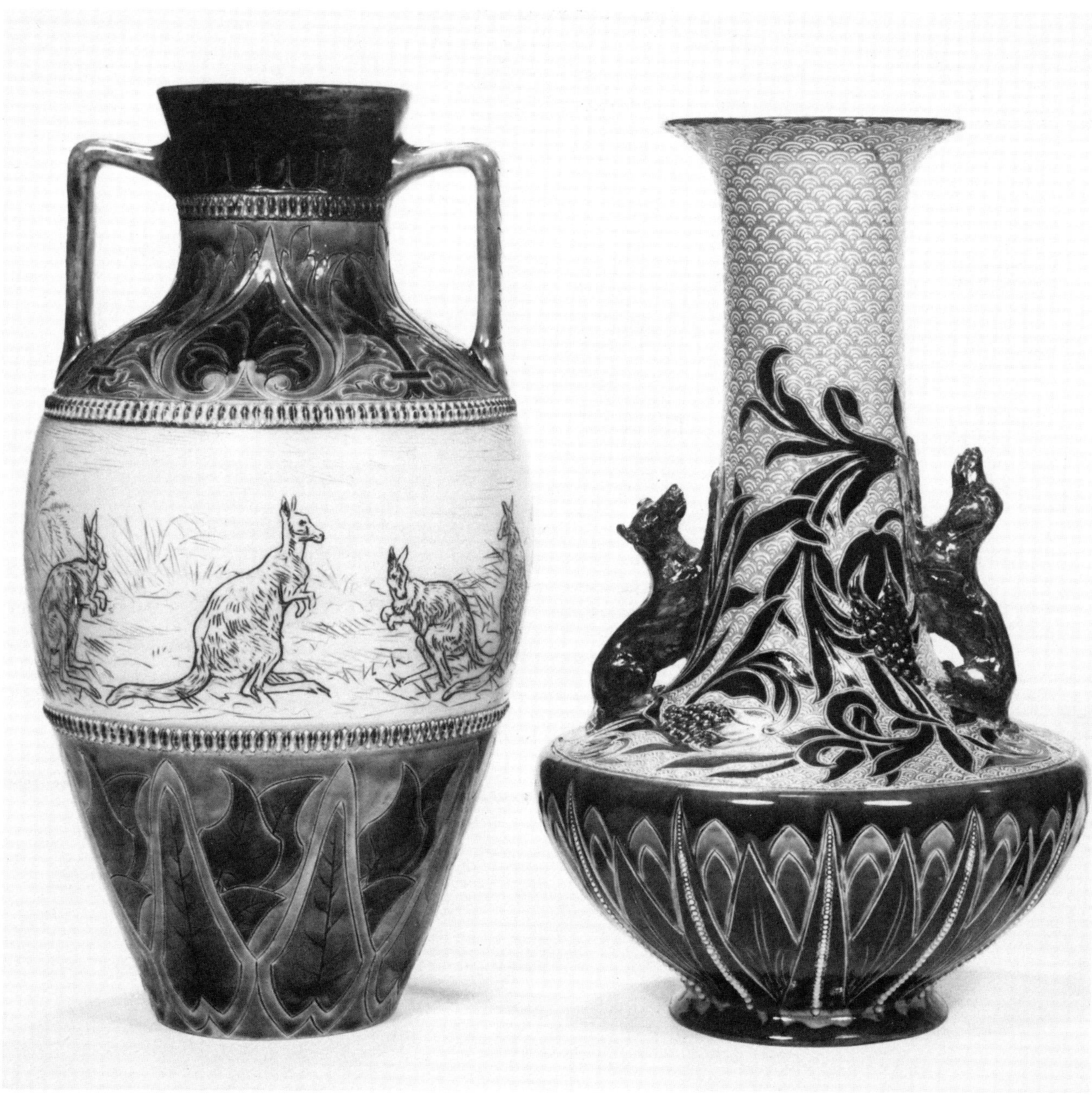

Figure 45: Vase with a continuous scene of kangaroos, borders by Annie Gentle and A.B., 1886, 14½in. Vase with dogs modelled in high relief and fruiting foliage, assistant's monogram A.B., 1889, 14in.

There was, however, criticism of the artistic quality of the pots from another quarter. Mark V Marshall, a designer of great originality and independence of thought, had joined Doulton & Co. in the late seventies after spending a frustrating apprenticeship with the Martin Brothers. He voiced his feelings in a seven stanza poem "Lambeth Laments", which roundly attacked the over-elaboration or "Roman splendours" as he termed it, which had become standard after the establishment of the studio system with its proliferation of assistants:

> "Away! bad dreams, oh: cease to care
> For Italy's voluptuous craze.
> Look back at Barlow's modest ways
> The love and zeal of early days,
> of Doulton Ware."[36]

Hannah as a "Head of Studio" must have read these comments and criticisms but appears to have been unaffected by them. Her own style continued virtually unchanged, inscribing in her preferred manner, horses, goats, cows, deer, oxen, sheep, rabbits, cats and dogs, mice, donkeys and all manner of domestic fowl, ducks, geese and so on. Occasionally more exotic creatures were introduced, taken from studies made at London Zoo and elsewhere: there were lions, elephants, hyenas, giraffes, kangaroos, all drawn with vigour and accuracy. Childen were associated with the animals in a natural way, usually in a happy relationship, unless frightened by geese or chased by a dog. Although John Sparkes in his second Society of Arts lecture voiced some criticism of her use of humans, the examples which have survived are successfully achieved and delightful in feeling.

The most unfortunate aspect of the studio system for Hannah was the virtual abandonment of any concern for the overall design of the piece. Her attention was confined solely to the reserved panel or frieze left after the decoration of the remaining part of the vase had been done by others. Various assistants worked on the backgrounds but frequently another artist decorator collaborated on virtually an equal footing. The association with Florence has already been noted, but in addition the deaf and dumb decorator Frank Butler became linked with Hannah — an association which continued well into the twentieth century.

For a three year period from 1882-1885 one of Hannah's older sisters, Lucy, was employed as a decorator. Her work is nearly always associated with either Hannah or Florence and usually takes the form of broadly massed foliate shapes. Lucy's decision to join Doulton & Co. may have been associated with the illness and death of Mrs Barlow at the age of sixty six in November 1882. The death of their devoted mother must have affected them deeply for she had shouldered all the family responsibilities since her husband's death. Through her own writings, for she was a prolific poet, it is possible to gain some insight into her fine character. Her will demonstrates how

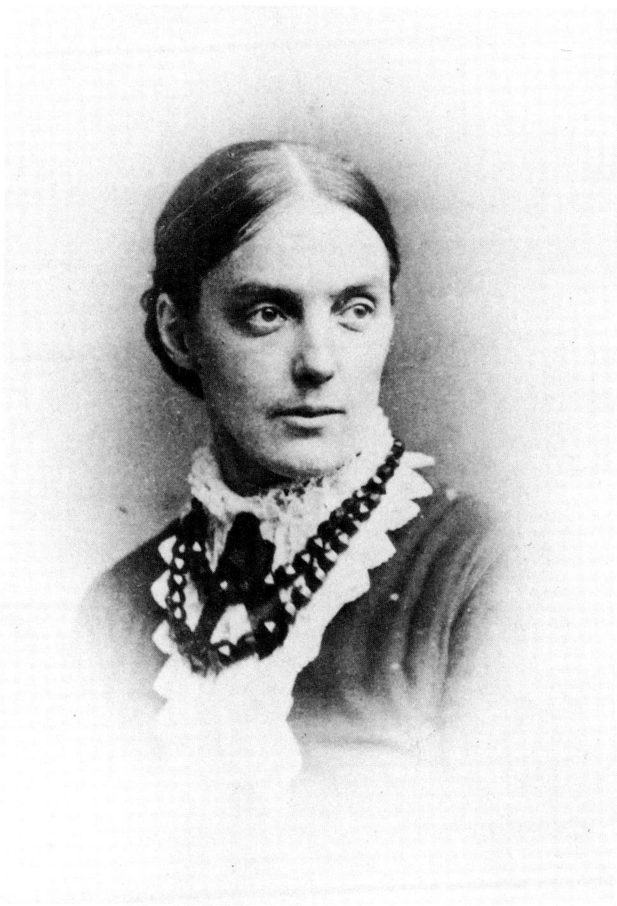

Figure 46: Lucy A. Barlow, Jan. 9th, 1880.

carefully she considered her children's welfare, leaving the bulk of her estate to those unmarried daughters who were not in employment and therefore dependant on receiving some income. The value of the estate was a little over four thousand pounds, just sufficient to provide a small income for the dependant daughters.

Lucy Barlow's association with Doulton & Co. had ceased by the mid-eighties. By then both Hannah and Florence were in their thirties and likely to remain spinsters; they were well established and happy in their careers. Lucy was therefore invited to become their housekeeper, an arrangement which, according to a family source, continued until their deaths. Hannah was now famous enough to be featured in special articles in *Queen* and *The Lady* ; the latter

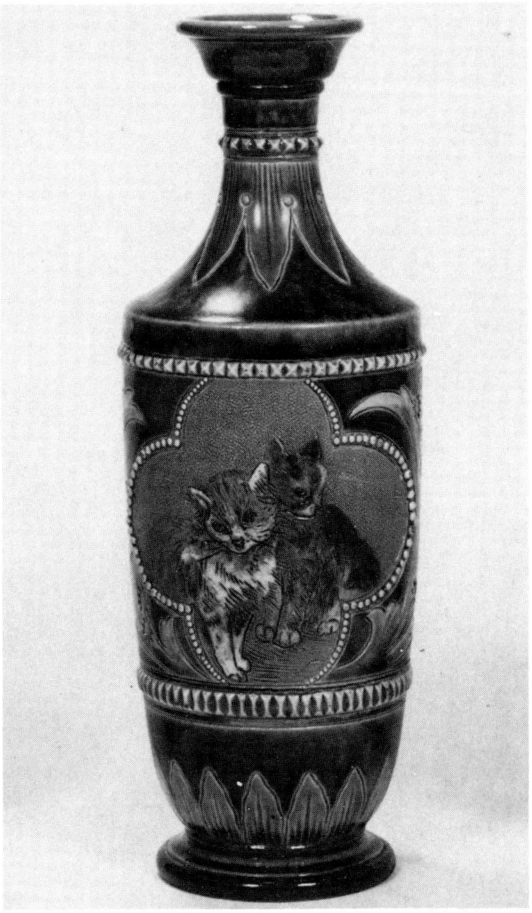

Figure 47: Vase with pâte-sur-pâte kittens, c. 1895, 10in.

described her strange assortment of animals in her private menagerie at Fern Cottage, Wraysbury:

"The latest addition is a little fox, just brought from South Wales, which was at first very savage, but is now both tame and gentle and follows Miss Barlow about as quietly as a well-trained dog."[37]

On one occasion, according to another family source, Irlam on a visit to his sisters was severely bitten on the calf by the fox which had been lurking unseen beneath the sofa.

The Lady also lists the various galleries in which Hannah was exhibiting, including the Dudley Gallery, Society of British Artists, and various provincial galleries including the Walker Art Gallery in Liverpool. In 1881 the Royal Academy accepted a terra-cotta relief entitled "Our Pet" and for most of the next ten years exhibited one or two of her clay relief models in the Summer Exhibition. The last to be shown was "So near and yet so far", a dog gazing wistfully at a cat in a tree (Plate 65). Florence was twice successful with watercolours, "A Young Adventurer" in the 1884 Academy and "Canaries" in 1885. In the article the two sisters are portrayed sharing a studio, working in perfect harmony, assured, successful and contented (Figure 49). A review in the "Frankfurter Zeitung"[38] refers to the stately and elegant appearance of the Doulton buildings which, if it was not for the utilitarian character of their surroundings, could be mistaken for palaces. The conditions of work in the studios were a cause of admiration and even amazement: the reporter is "completely bewildered and overcome" but nevertheless responds most strongly to "the charming groups of animals designed by Miss Hannah Barlow . . . She does not require many lines in order to give her animals character — just a few strokes suffice. Her designs remind one in this respect of the charming Japanese drawings."[39]

The same issue of Studio Notes which carried extracts from the newspaper article has an amusing spoof programme for an evening variety

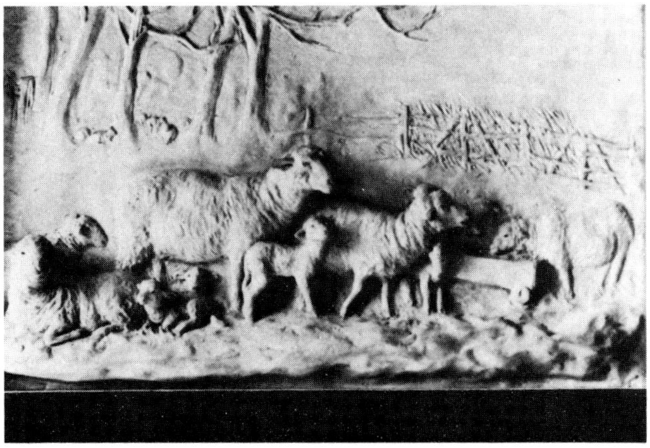

Figure 48: 'Sheep in meadow' modelled terracotta, c. 1885.

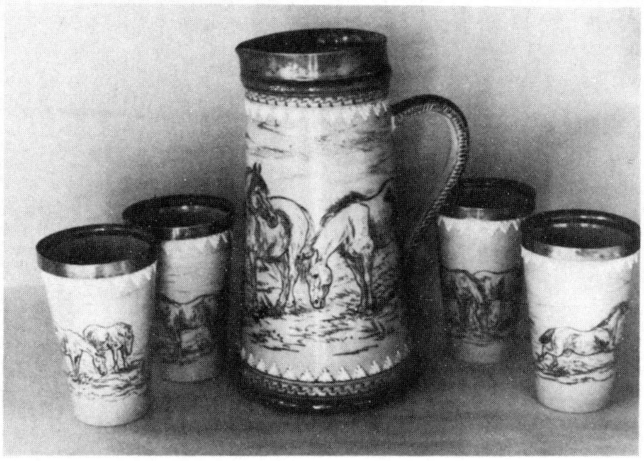

Figure 49: Set of Lemonade Jug and four beakers, 1878.

entertainment, supposedly to be given by Doulton employees: "During the interval, Miss Barlow will introduce her performing dog and her wonderful Dead Cat, Mr Tinworth will exhibit his clever mice."[40] A piece in the Pall Mall Gazette [41] reinforces the picture of a marvellously civilised and culturally rich working environment. It describes dining rooms, a library, museum rooms for study, relatively short working hours (nine to five), a sick fund and a self-governing committee to deal with any quarrels between the workers. Not surprisingly application for places in the studios far exceeded their capacity to take on new recruits, particularly as so very few chose to leave.

One of the most enlightened features of the regime at Doulton & Co. was the institution of an annual fortnight's holiday for all taken in August. In 1886 Hannah and Florence decided to spend their holiday together in a shepherd's cottage in a quiet part of Surrey. They set off together with their sketching gear and a large hamper of provisions, first by train and then by waggonette: "the country grew wilder and wilder", they began to think that their driver had made a mistake and that they were lost; eventually as evening drew in they arrived at their destination, a "very rustic" cottage standing on its own in the middle of a field. They awoke next morning to "a great noise" which turned out to be a reception committee of forty geese under their window: "We felt the day had begun well with a welcome from so many friends." Each day

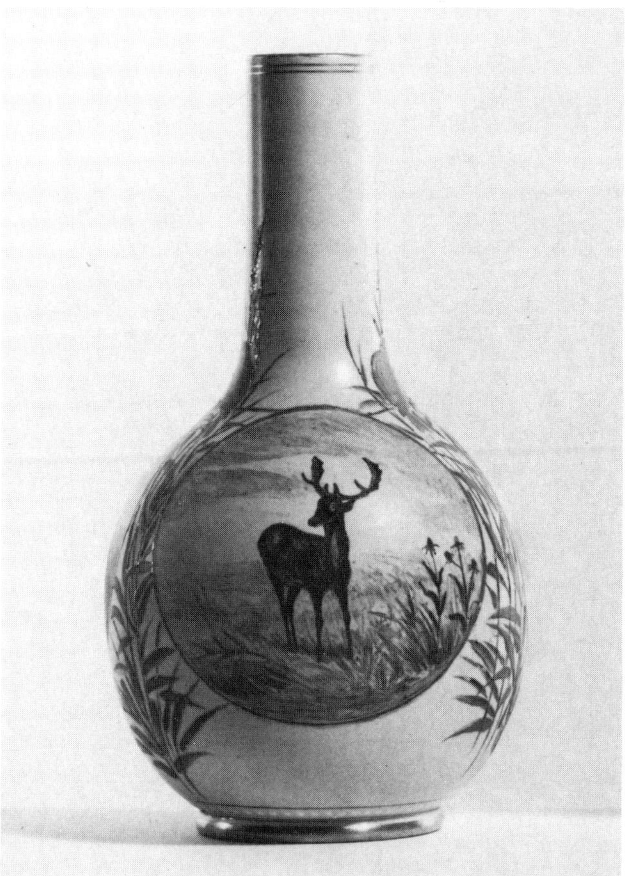

Figure 50: Carrara vase painted with three panels of deer divided by birds sitting on rushes, painted by Florence Barlow, c. 1890, 11½ in.

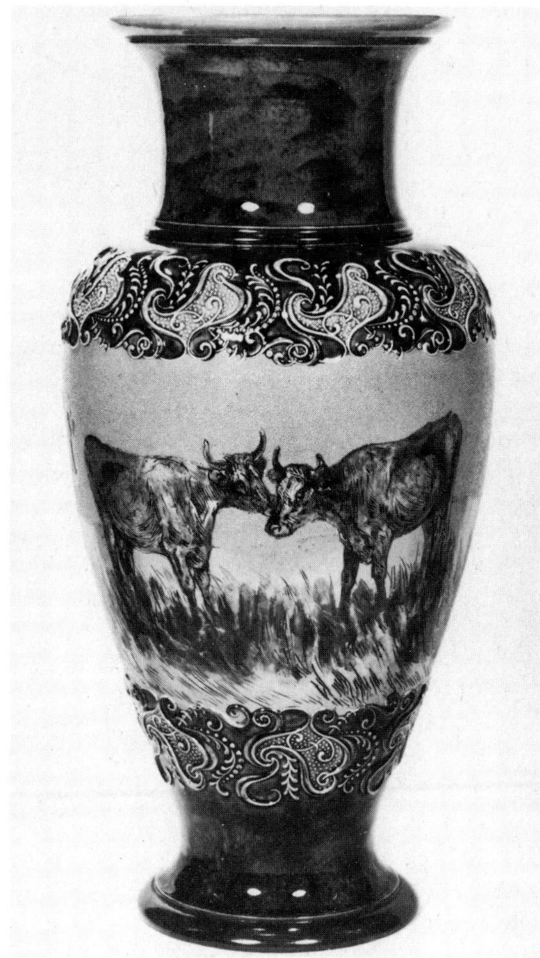

Figure 51: Vase with a frieze of cattle in pâte-sur-pâte, borders by Florence Roberts, c. 1895, 18½ in.

after breakfast they went out sketching, returning in the evening for a supper prepared by "a cheerful little soul" of a housekeeper. Their interest in the domestic livestock at the farm nearby was more than matched by the animals' interest in them. They were no sooner settled down sketching than their work was interrupted by a "brood of little pigs which came round to have a look at us and to shake our easels by rubbing their little fat sides against them." Their "sedate manners" impressed the locals who assumed that they were much older and able to recall events such as the Coronation of William the Fourth, long before they were born; but no offence was caused. At the end of their stay they regretfully said goodbye to their new friends: "The two blind pigs, numerous cows and calves, horses etc., and the rough old sheepdog which used to invite himself to dinner sometimes."[42]

Both sisters were regular contributors to the "Studio Notes" which appeared every two or three months from 1883—1892, remaining loyal to the editor Walter Gandy even when others defected. The next issue after the one which contained the account by Hannah of the sisters' country holiday included a ghost story written by Florence. It was a singularly inept and tedious piece extending to over five chapters, amateur in the worst sense. The editor in a laudable attempt to raise standards published an independent critical evaluation of the piece which was cruelly hostile: "The story . . . has evidently been written in a great hurry . . . consequently (there are) many errors of grammar, punctuation, expression. The descriptions are diffuse, and the dramatic element has not been made at all effective."[43] Not surprisingly the editor reported that he was "getting a little disheartened" at the lack of response. Various schemes were tried to keep the idea of a regular "house magazine" going, including appointing an editorial committee of five, and spacing out the issue to allow more time for the preparation of each number. Hannah continued to provide water-colour sketches and Florence, not discouraged by criticism, contributed occasional illustrated articles. These included a piece on a visit to the Crystal Palace Bird Show in 1891 — "Whilst sketching the nightingale I was questioned by a lady why I cared 'to copy that plain-coloured bird, when there were so many prettier ones' (which did it matter to her?) I told her I sketched it because they are rarely to be seen."[44]

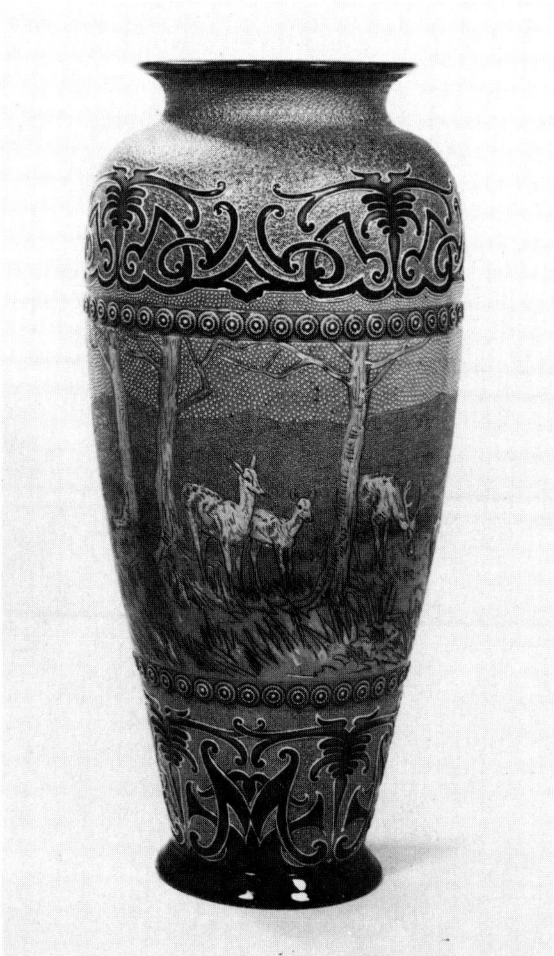

Figure 52: Vase with deer in a mountain landscape, borders by Florence Barlow, c. 1895, 17¼ in.

6. THE NINETIES ONWARDS

In retrospect those still working for Doulton & Co. in the middle and late nineties must have viewed the previous decade as a golden age of prosperity. Employment at the Art Pottery had continued to expand through the eighties; in 1890 almost three hundred and fifty artists and assistants were employed, twice as many as ten years earlier. These high numbers were sustained for the first part of the nineties but, by the turn of the century, they were beginning to diminish until, by the time of Hannah's retirement, in 1913, they were down to less than one hundred.

In 1887 Henry Doulton was knighted in recognition of his great services to art and industry. A severe fire at the works at the end of the following year caused considerable damage, destroying the major part of the Lambeth works. Rebuilding began virtually immediately and within ten months production was back to normal. The company was able to triumph over such misfortunes on the wave of confidence generated by the critical and popular approval accorded to the series of ambitious displays at exhibitions in London, Manchester, Glasgow and elsewhere.

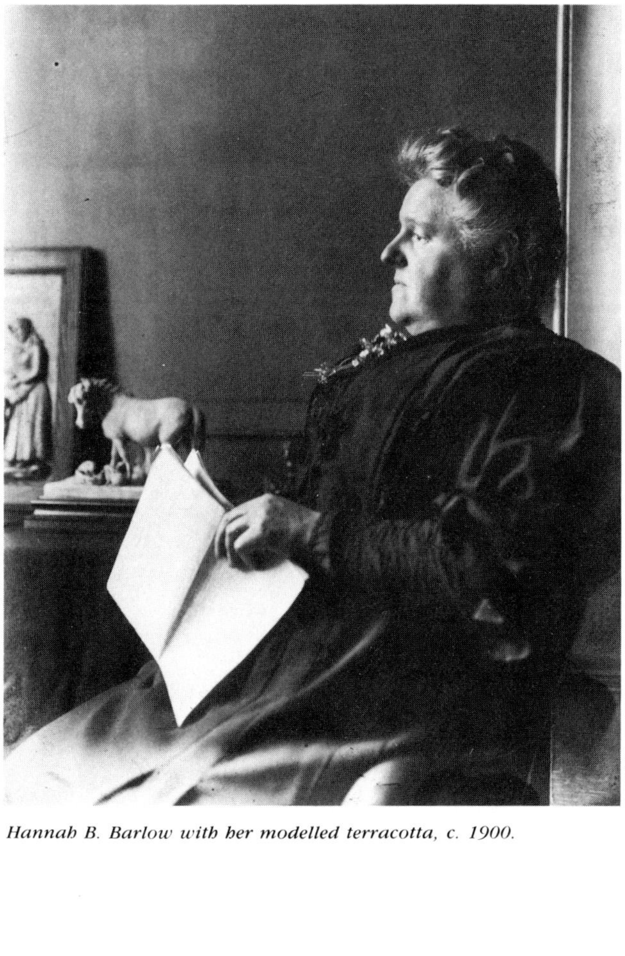

Hannah B. Barlow with her modelled terracotta, c. 1900.

In 1890 a strike of throwers disrupted production for three months. The dispute was about the employment of apprentices whom the workers saw as a threat to their own jobs. Henry Doulton was deeply offended, for it seemed to him that the men were striking against their own fellows. The dispute was waged ruthlessly by the workers who were aiming to bring the entire company to a halt. Their cause attracted little outside sympathy and eventually they surrendered completely. It was then Henry Doulton's turn to be ruthless, refusing to employ the bulk of strikers ever again. The editor of Studio Notes was at this time Joseph H. Mott, later to succeed Rix as Art Director of the Pottery. While considering that particular strike to be a lost cause he appears to sympathise with the use of the strike weapon: "My own opinion of a strike is that under certain conditions it may be the best and only way for labour to bring about an adjustment of its relations to Capital; to procure an equitable and just recognition by Capital of the part which labour plays in the Country's commerce."[45] The views of the lady artists on these profound and contentious issues are unfortunately not recorded; however, in that same issue of Studio Notes, appeared the piece by Florence on the Crystal Palace bird show already quoted. Hannah contributed two watercolours entitled "Homewards" and "Meditation", suggesting that the even tenor of their lives was unaffected by the turmoil surrounding them.

Throughout the nineties and indeed until the end of Hannah's active involvement in the decoration of pottery, the standard subjects of domestic livestock and pets, with occasionally more exotic imports, continued to be used in the traditional way. The rheumatism which had affected her earlier, requiring her to use her left hand in preference to her right one, may well be a cause of the poor quality of drawing found in some of these later pieces. A more likely explanation is that, after upwards of thirty years producing roughly one thousand different designs each year, understandably her enthusiasm and freshness of vision was fading. High quality pieces were produced, however, particularly when the approach was changed: a number of ambitious faience vases and tile panels in the nineties (Plates 61,62), show well the painterly techniques of her watercolour sketches (carried out as relaxation and regularly included in Studio Notes) translated into the novel medium. She also became involved in "Carrara" and "Crown Lambeth Ware": the latter was a particularly refined and expensive form of faience, examples of

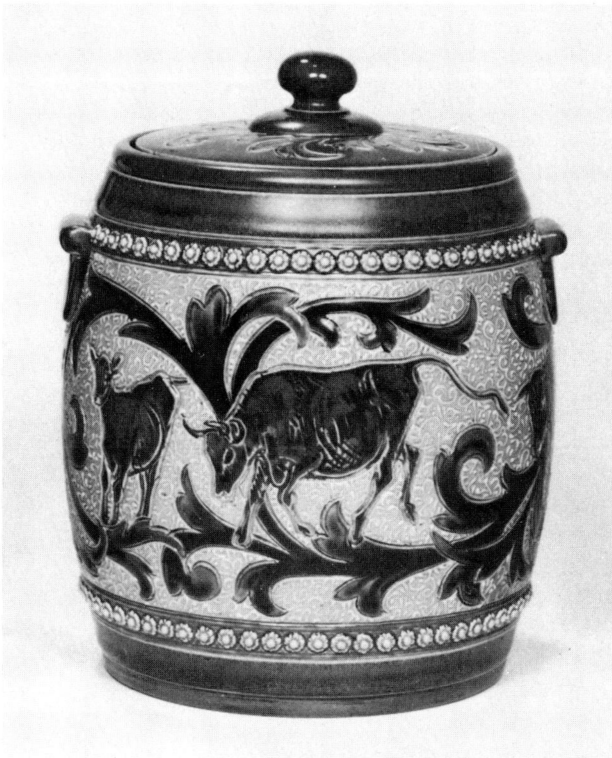

Figure 54: Tobacco jar with cows frolicking amongst foliate scrolls by Eliza Simmance, c. 1895, 6½ in.

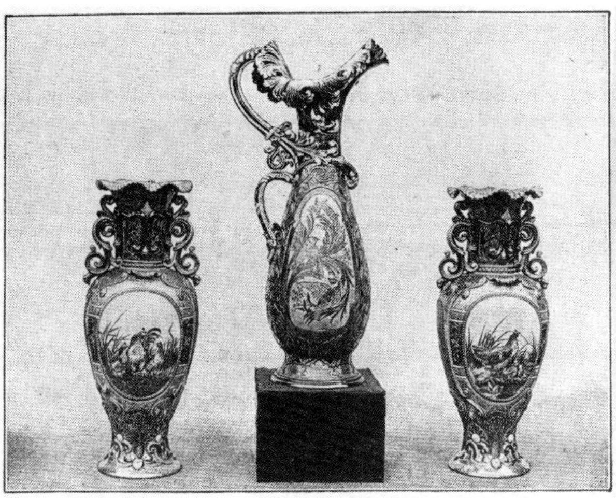

Figure 55: Vases by Mark Marshall with panels decorated by Florence Barlow, shown at the Chicago World's Fair 1893.

which were shown at the Chicago fair of 1893. Due to heavy kiln losses, for the technique was extremely delicate and required repeated firings, it was considered to be "the worst loss maker of all the Lambeth Wares"[46] and production was discontinued after ten years.

Florence also changed, but by fundamentally altering her approach to design: in addition to the naturalistic pâte-sur-pâte birds, which she continued with until the end of her career, she adopted formalised bird-like swirling patterns using the newly introduced tube-lining then becoming fashionable in several art potteries. These designs owe something to the Art Nouveau forms which Eliza Simmance, Mark Marshall, Frances Pope and others were evolving at the same time.

A great effort was made to produce a magnificent display for the Chicago World's Fair of 1893. Many ambitious exhibition pieces were specially made for it. Mark Marshall in particular, having apparently forgotten his strictures on "Roman Splendour", produced pieces of the utmost elaboration, some on a massive scale. In certain pieces he collaborated with Florence, somewhat overwhelming her pâte-sur-pâte birds with his roccoco surrounds (Figure 55). It was all a far cry from the old style; the direct simplicity of salt-glaze had disappeared and been replaced with an over-loading of ornament. Not surprisingly perhaps, the Art Journal, after having featured the pieces in an article pre-viewing the show, awarded "place of honour" to the Worcester Royal Porcelain Company for its even more intricate but "delicate as lace" pierced ware.

Sir Henry Doulton, who considered his firm second-to-none, must have been greatly chagrined by the Art Journal judgement. He was now in his mid-seventies and in failing health, no longer able to keep a personal eye on all his multifarious and still prospering enterprises. Hannah wrote to Gosse after his death in 1897: "Of late years, it was not possible for him to be such a constant visitor to the studios. Since he has ceased to come, we have missed him very much. My sister Florence agrees with me that some of the pleasantest memories of our life are of the days when we began the decoration work upon the stoneware, and with them the eager and generous sympathy of Sir Henry Doulton is indissolubly connected."[47]

The story of the slow decline of the Lambeth Art Pottery after Sir Henry Doulton's death is fully told in Desmond Eyles "The Doulton Lambeth Wares". Although, inevitably linked with Hannah and Florence's employment by Royal Doulton, as it became after 1902, little emerges to enrich our understanding of how the pair of sisters worked in their remaining years at the pottery. The work they did in the early twentieth century continued with well tried past techniques: occasionally pieces of high quality were produced but it appears that many fewer pieces were made than in the heyday of the Art Studios. Family accounts of visits to the sisters in their comfortable retirement paint a picture of contentment

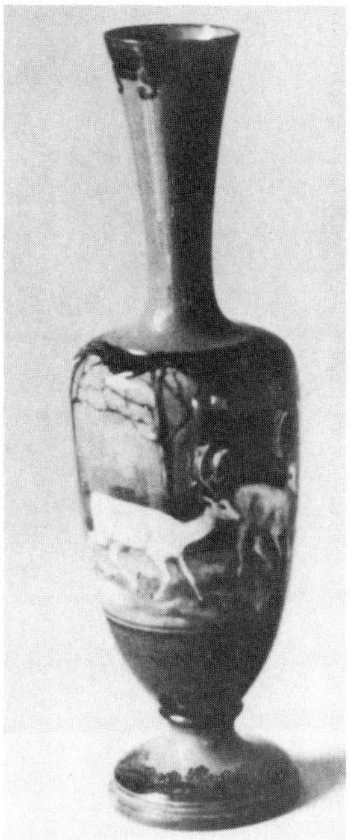

Figure 56: Crown Lambeth vase painted with deer, c. 1901.

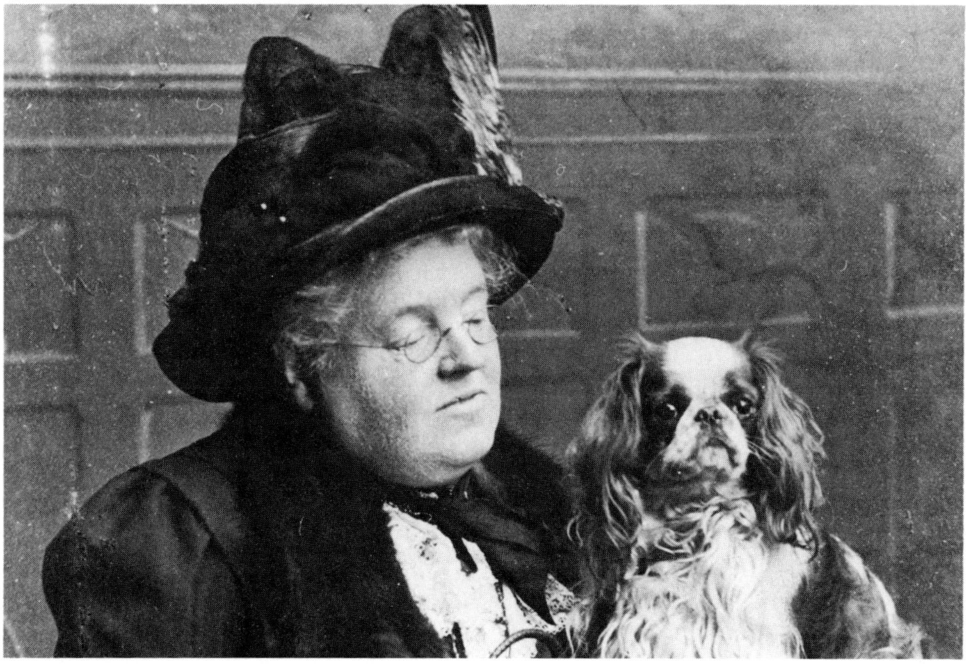

Figure 57: Hannah B. Barlow & Rufus Darwin, February 1913.

and reasonable affluence, surrounded by domestic animals of all sorts. Hannah had always been close to her brother Irlam and when she died on November 16th, 1916, she left her possessions to him. He had been bankrupted in the nineties and, like her mother perhaps, Hannah bestowed benefit where it was most needed. She possessed great kindness and virtue, but in addition a rare talent which found its perfect expression (and time) in the Lambeth Art Studios' enterprise. Her name will always be identified with Doulton pottery, and her many thousands of decorative designs will remain a permanent source of delight to all who value brilliant technique, originality and great charm.

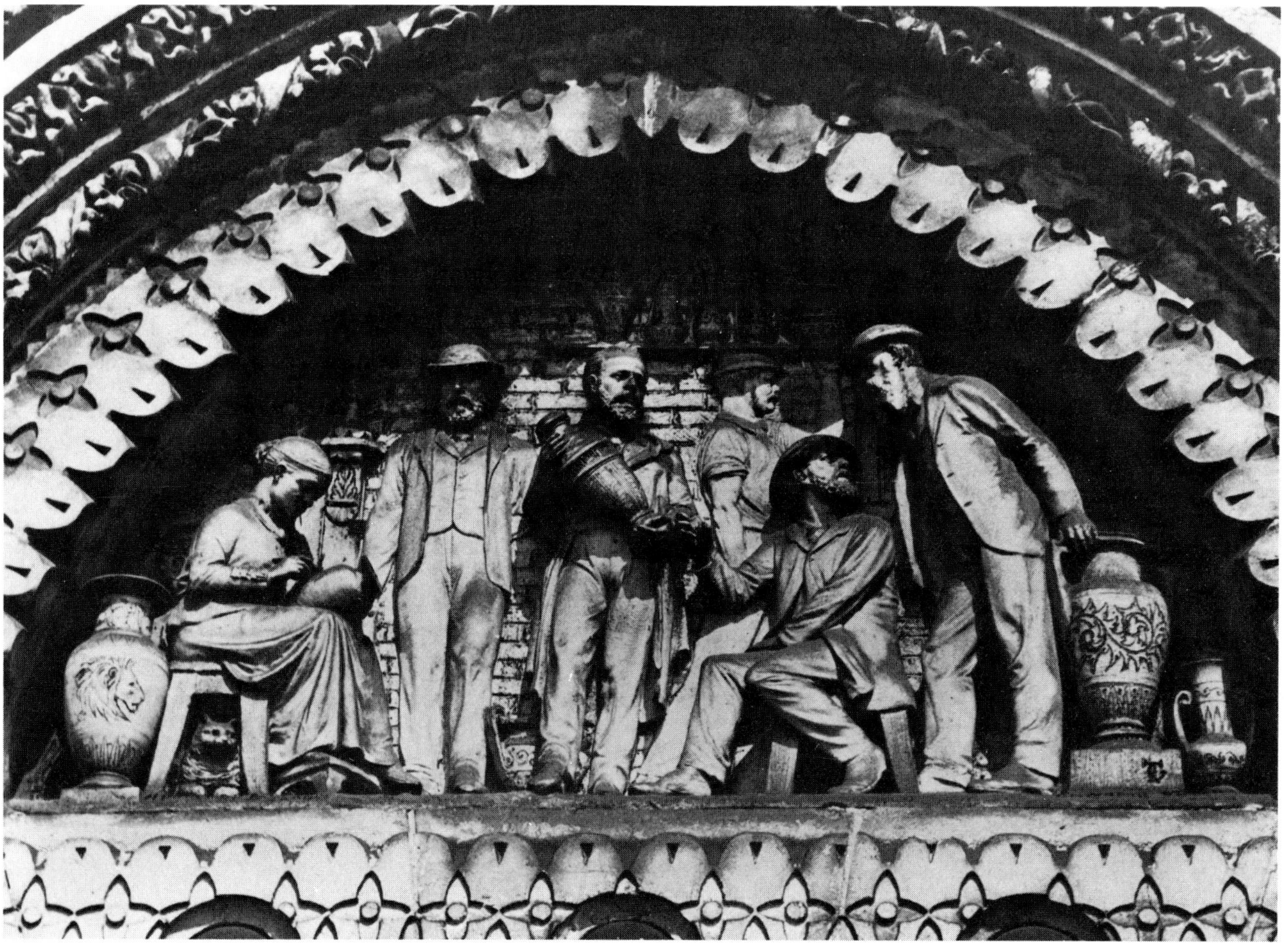

Figure 59: A terracotta panel modelled by George Tinworth, c. 1876, depicting Henry Doulton surrounded by some of his leading artists, including Hannah Barlow and her cat. The panel is still in position above the main door of the old headquarters building in Lambeth High Street.

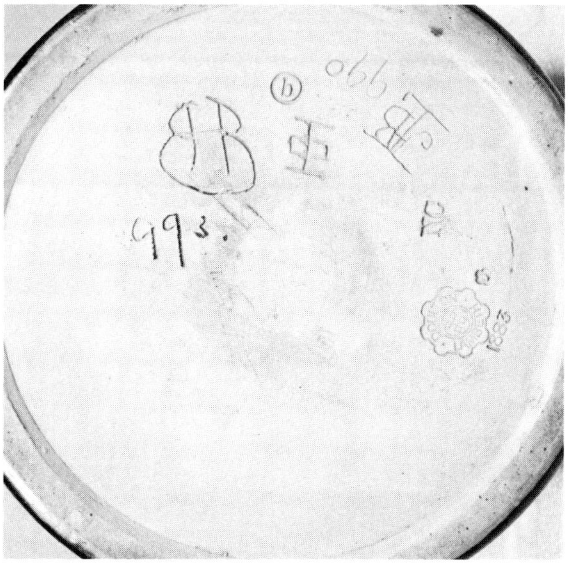

Figure 60: Hannah and Lucy Barlows' incised monograms.

The author wishes to thank the following for their assistance in his research: Mrs Margaret Barlow, Lt. Col. Kenneth Barlow, Desmond Eyles, Albert Gallichan, Lady Muriel Herbert, Louise Irvine, Mrs Ann Montgomery, the Chichester Museum, Royal Doulton Archives, Brighton Polytechnic library.

Photographs by courtesy of:
Royal Doulton Tableware PLC — Figure 8.
Harriman-Judd Collection, Los Angeles — Figures 5,12,13,14,19,25-32,34.
Victoria & Albert Museum — Figure 33.

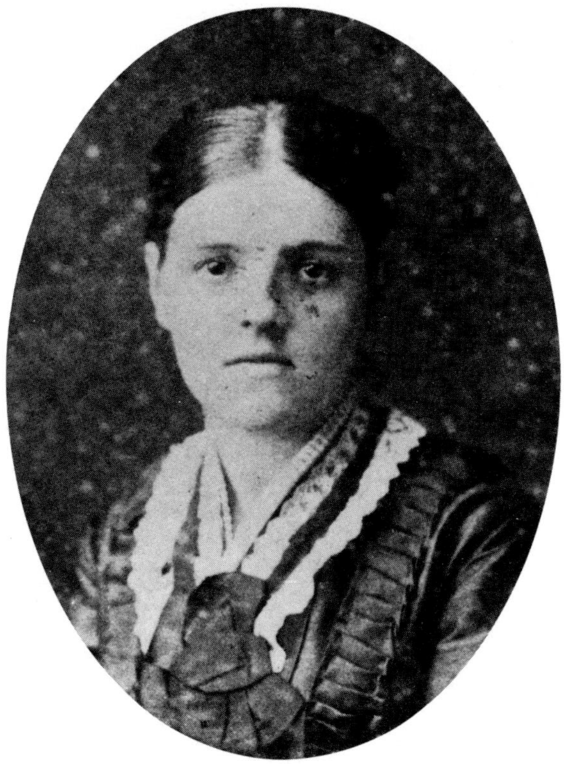

Figure 58: Hannah B. Barlow, July 1877.

NOTES

1. *Memoire of Arthur Bolton Barlow by his Mother:* privately printed, October, 1879.
2. Ibid: p. 28.
3. Ibid: p. 7 & 8.
4. Ibid: p. 14.
5. Ibid: p. 18.
6. Ibid: p. 17 & 18.
7. Two sketchbooks are in the possession of the Royal Doulton archive; both have the address of 48, South Lambeth Road inside the cover and contain numerous sketches made at dates between 1871 & 1873.
8. *Lady Artists: Miss Hannah Bolton Barlow,* The Lady, 24 March 1887, p. 215.
9. See *Angel in the Studio,* by Anthea Callen, Astragal Books, 1979, p. 92, note 33, for speculation on whether the sculptor W.G. Rogers was in fact Alfred Rogers.
10. *Memoire,* op. cit., p. 16.
11. *A Critical Essay on the Life and Works of George Tinworth,* by Edmund W. Gosse, Fine Art Society, 1883, p. 8.
12. See *George Tinworth,* by Peter Rose, C.D.N. Corp. Los Angeles, 1982, for a detailed account of Tinworth's career.
13. One of the more preposterous recommendations to come out of a Government inquiry into the problem of the superfluity of women students, was the suggestion that only unattractive women who were unlikely to find marriage partners should be recruited to the Schools.
14. *Notes on Lambeth Stoneware etc.,* by John C.L. Sparkes, Doulton & Co. 1880, p. 32.
15. Ibid: p. 31.
16. *Staffordshire Pots & Pottery* by G. Woolliscroft Rhead & Frederick Alfred Rhead, Hutchinson & Co. 1906, p. 351.
17. Ibid: p. 355.
18. Ibid: p. 355 & 356.
19. The scrapbook contains hundreds of assorted drawings and paintings mostly dating from the 1870s. It is in the possession of the Harriman-Judd Collection, Los Angeles U.S.A.
20. *Sir Henry Doulton* by Edmund Gosse, edited by Desmond Eyles, Hutchinson 1970, p. 181.
21. Ibid: p. 81.
22. Ibid: p. 81.
23. *Studio Notes* No. 3 edited by Walter Gandy, April 1884. A manuscript compilation of original contributions from subscribing employees of the Art Pottery Studios, who also constituted its readership: a prototype of the modern "house magazine".
24. Ibid: p. 9 & 10.
25. Over the four year period in which the Annual International Exhibitions were held, public support waned and an initial profit was turned into a cumulative loss of £150,000 by the end of the series.
26. *Studio Notes:* op cit., p. 5 & 6.
27. Ibid: p. 10.
28. Quoted in *The Doulton Lambeth Wares,* by Desmond Eyles, Hutchinson, 1975, p. 92.
29. *Doulton,* by Gosse; op. cit., p. 81.
30. Ibid: p. 82.
31. *Art Journal,* 1876, p. 250.
32. *Lambeth Stoneware,* by Rhoda Edwards. Borough of Lambeth 1973, Facsimile insert.
33. *Doulton* by Gosse; op. cit., p. 85.
34. *Studio Notes;* op. cit., p. 139.
35. A pair of faience vases decorated by Mary Arding and bearing the year stamp for 1880 have retained the original retailer's label: "The Old Pottery Galleries, Oxford St., 2.6.82, price 52/6d".
36. *Studio Notes,* op. cit., p. 92.
37. *The Lady;* op. cit., p. 215 & 216.
38. *Frankfurter Zeitung:* 26th November 1884: referred to in Studio Notes, No. 7, p. 146-149.
39. Ibid: p. 147.
40. Ibid: p. 159.
41. *Pall Mall Magazine*: 30th May 1884, *Women who work VIII Artists in Pottery & Glass.*
42. Studio Notes, No. 7 (New Series): 1886, p. 137-145
43. Studio Notes, No. 8 (New Series): 1886, p. 6 & 7.
44. Studio Notes, No. 10 (New Series): 1891, p. 143.
45. Ibid: p. 157.
46. *Lambeth Wares,* by Eyles: op. cit., p. 51.
47. *Doulton* by Gosse: op. cit., p. 182.

CATALOGUE OF EXHIBITION

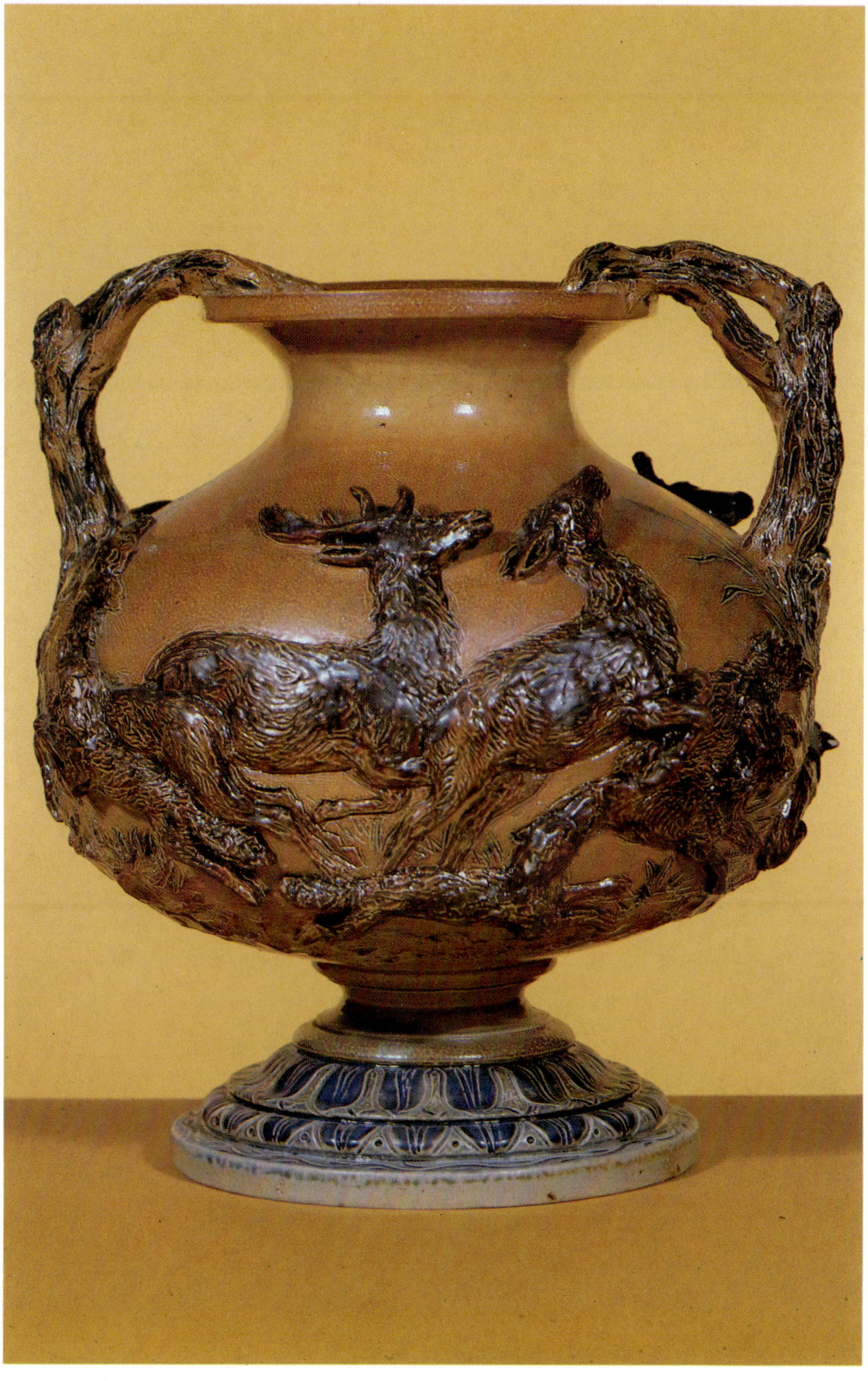

1. *Vase modelled in high relief with a continuous scene of wolves attacking deer, c. 1872, 11¼ in.*

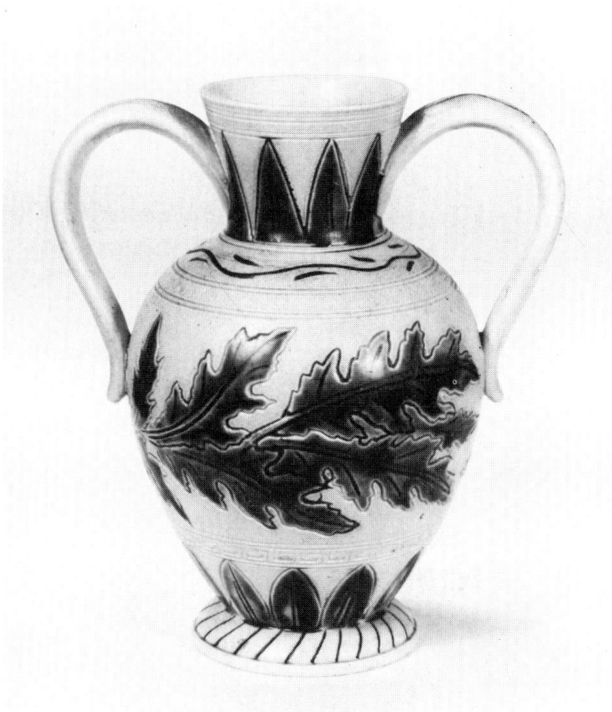

2. *An early vase with a band of blue glazed leaves, c. 1871, incised with the early monogram HBB, 6¼in.*

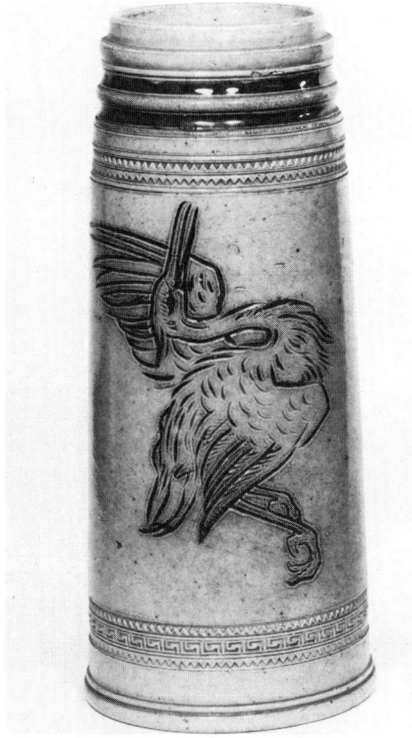

3. *Jug incised with a heron, the recesses filled with blue pigment, c. 1871, 10in.*

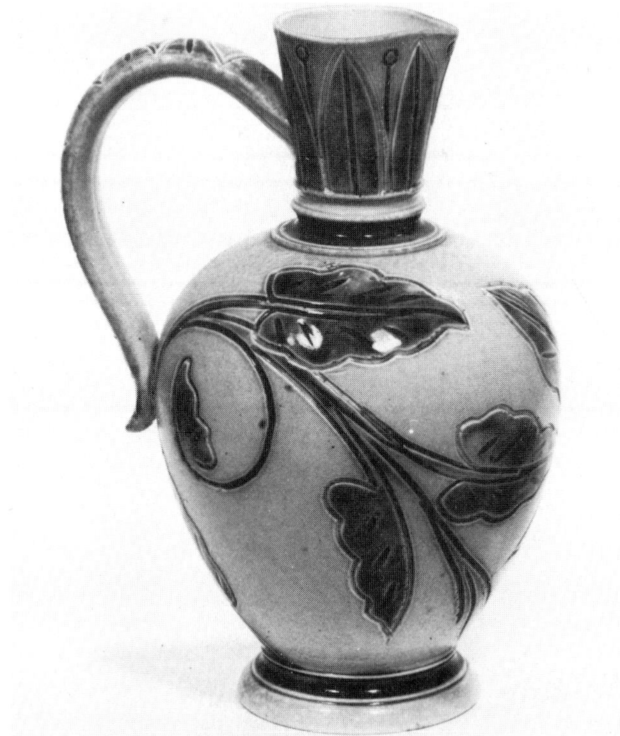

4. *Jug with blue glazed foliage on a white, body, c. 1871, 7½in.*

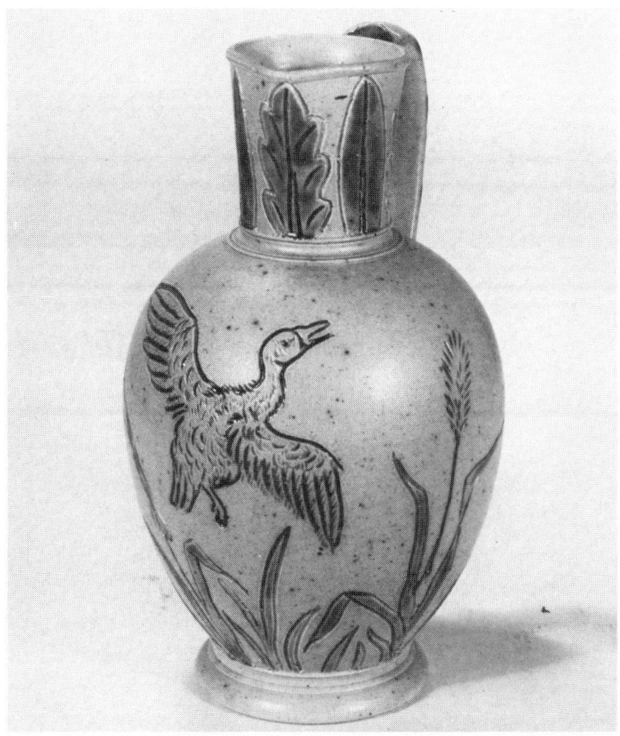

5. *Jug in pale blue clay with a duck in flight, c. 1871, 7¾in.*

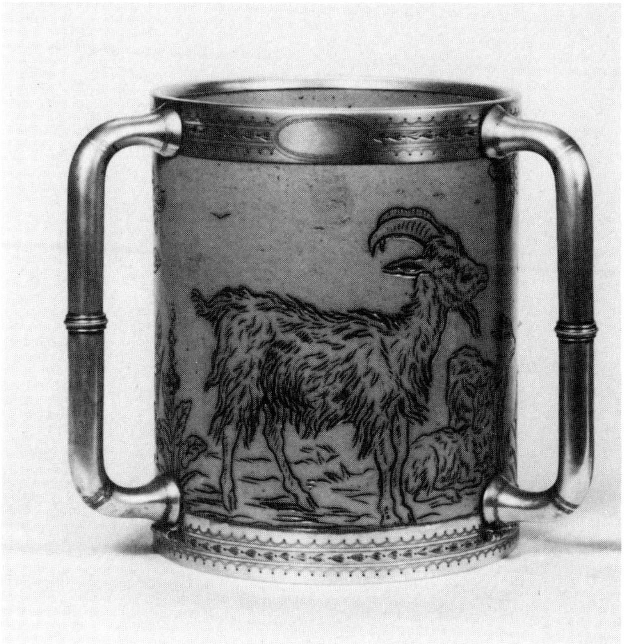

6. Massive loving cup with elaborate silver plated mounts, each panel with goats and kids, c. 1872, 8¼in.

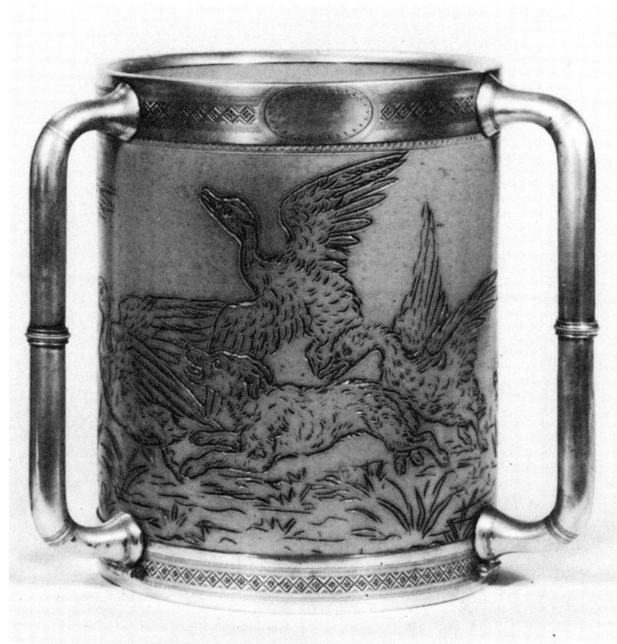

7. Massive loving cup with elaborate silver plated mounts with a dog scattering alarmed ducks, c. 1872, 8¾in.

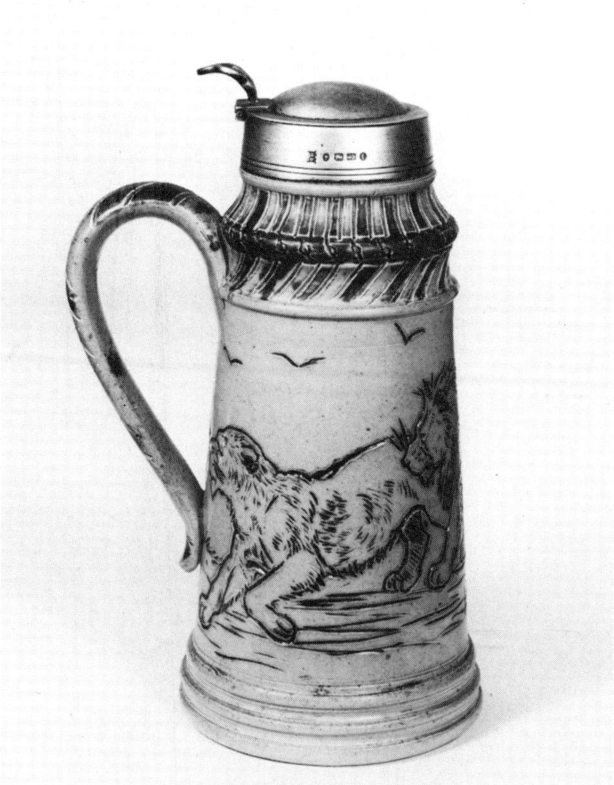

8. Silver mounted tankard with a lion and two lionesses, c. 1872, 9in.

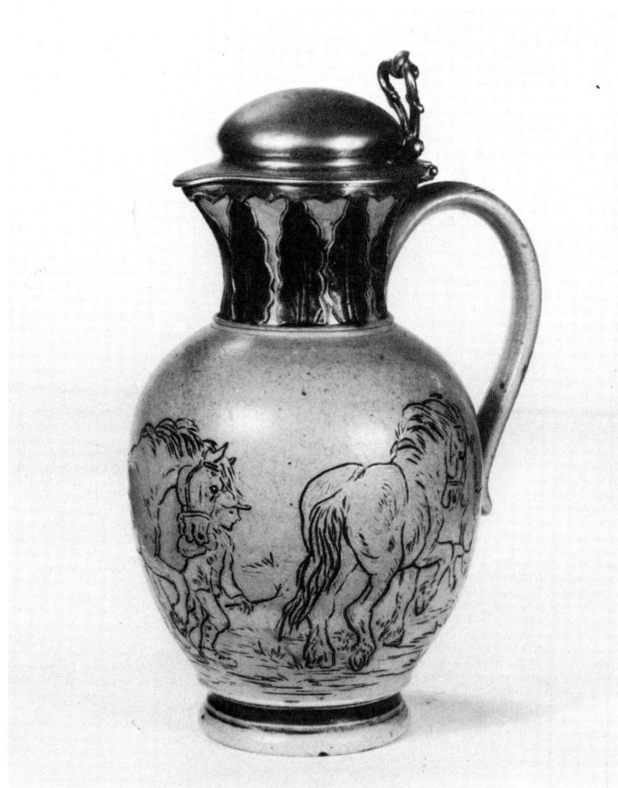

9. Silver mounted jug with farm horses being released in a field, c. 1872, 10in.

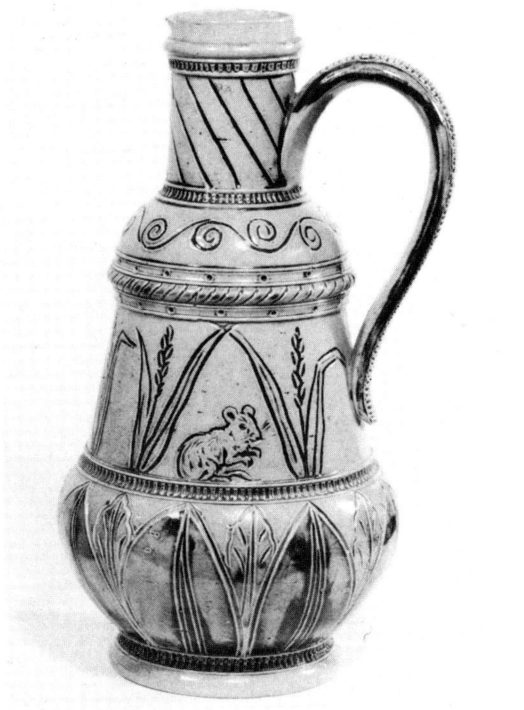

10. *Jug with mice, ears of corn and stiff leaves, c. 1872, 9¾in.*

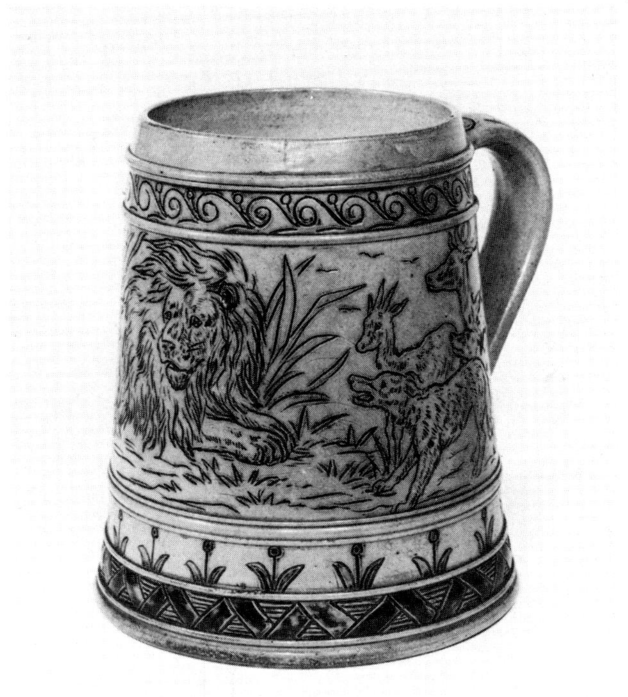

11. *Massive tankard with an assortment of animals paying homage to the king of the animals, the lion, c. 1872, 8¾in.*

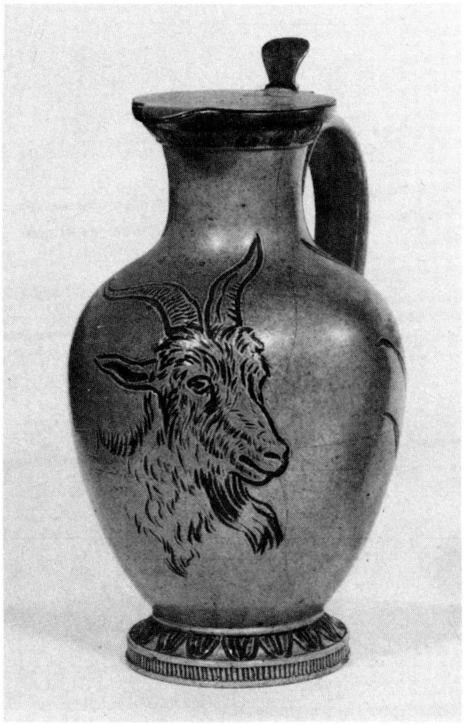

12. *Jug with a head of a billygoat, silver plated mounts, c. 1872, 9in.*

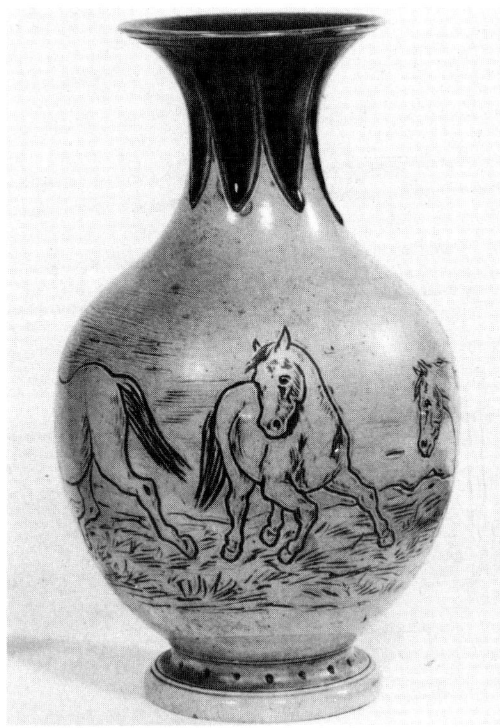

13. *Vase by Florence Barlow with running horses, 1874, 9½in.*

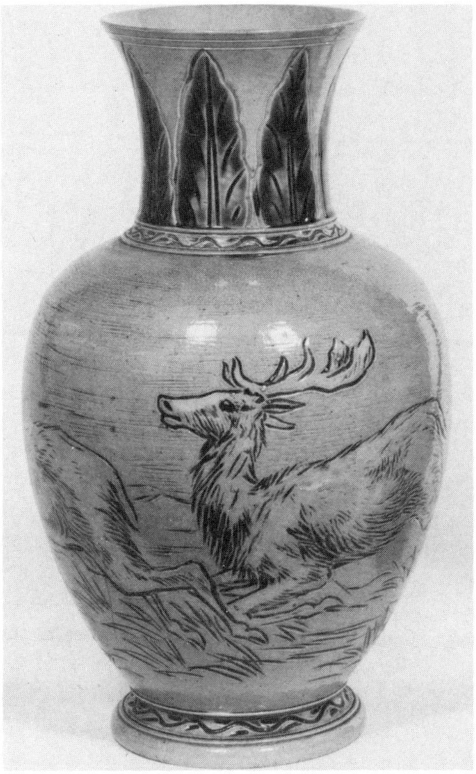

14. Vase with a continuous scene of running deer, 1873, 11½in.

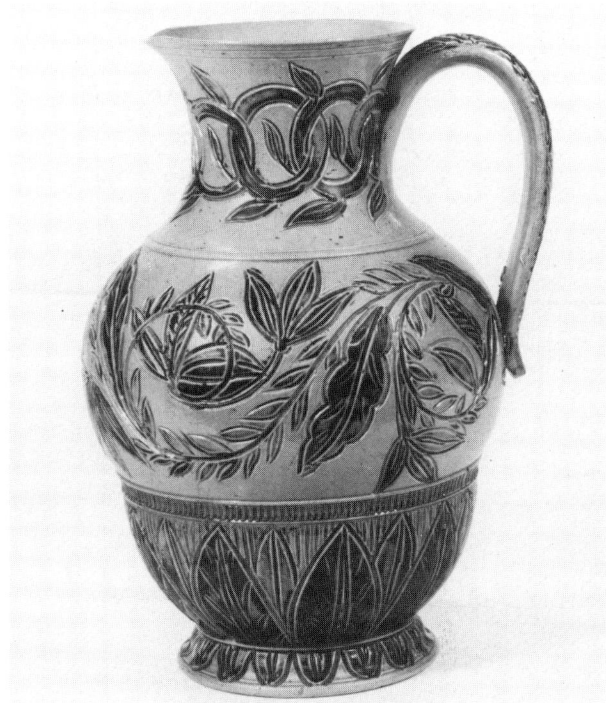

15. Jug with bands of foliage, 1873, 8½in.

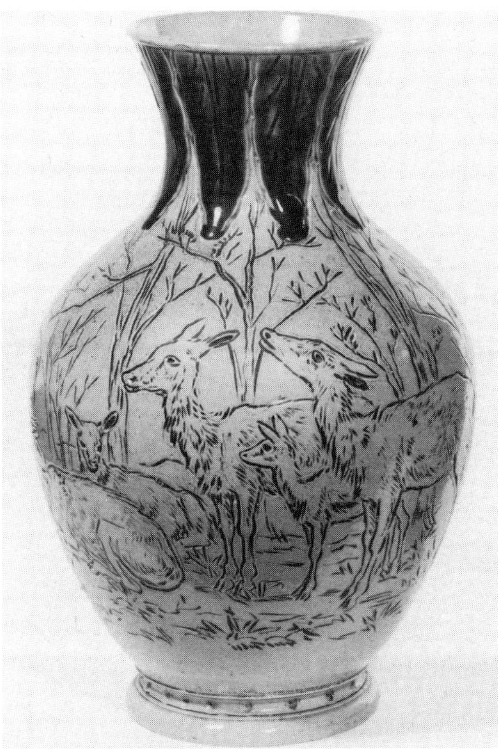

16. Vase with deer in a forest, 1873, 10½in.

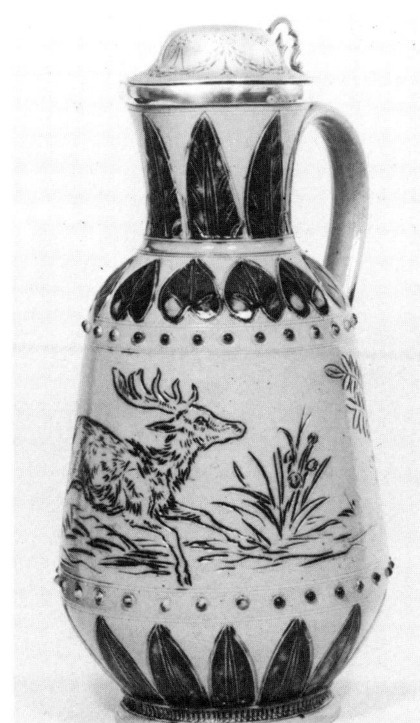

17. Lemonade Jug with a running stag, silver mounts, 1873, 14in.

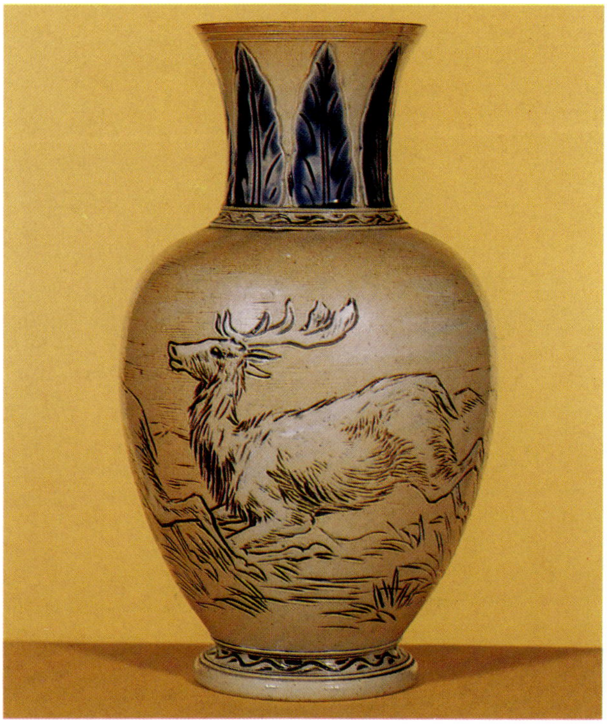

18. *Vase with running deer, 1873, 11¼ in.*

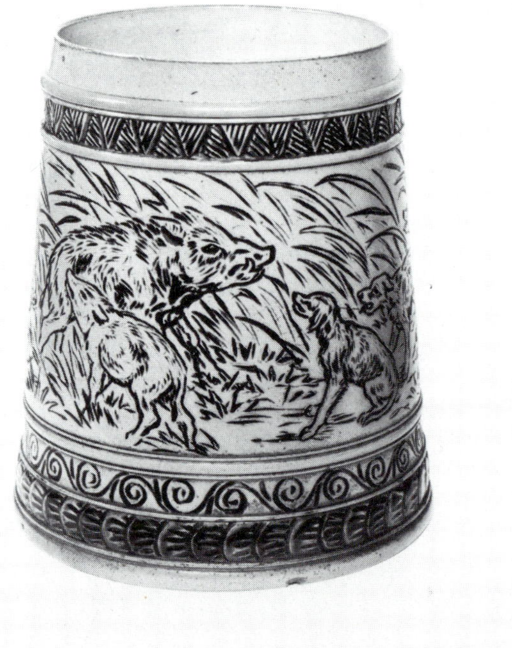

19. *Massive tankard with a pair of dogs attacking wild boar, 1874, 9in.*

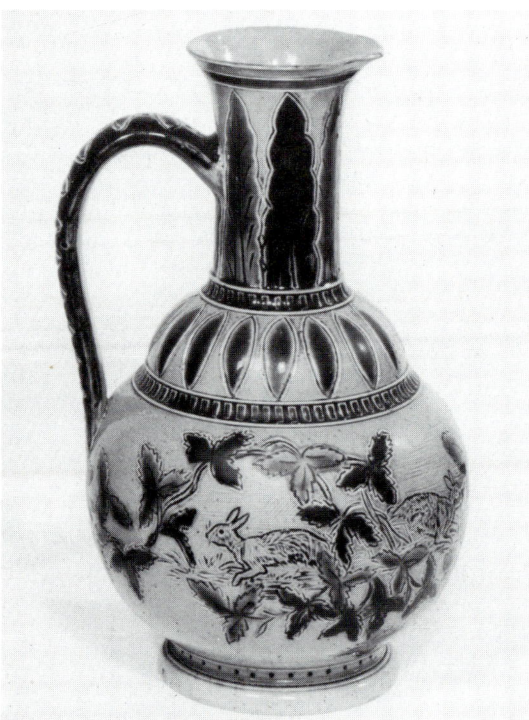

20. *Jug with rabbits amongst foliage by Florence Barlow, 1874, 9in.*

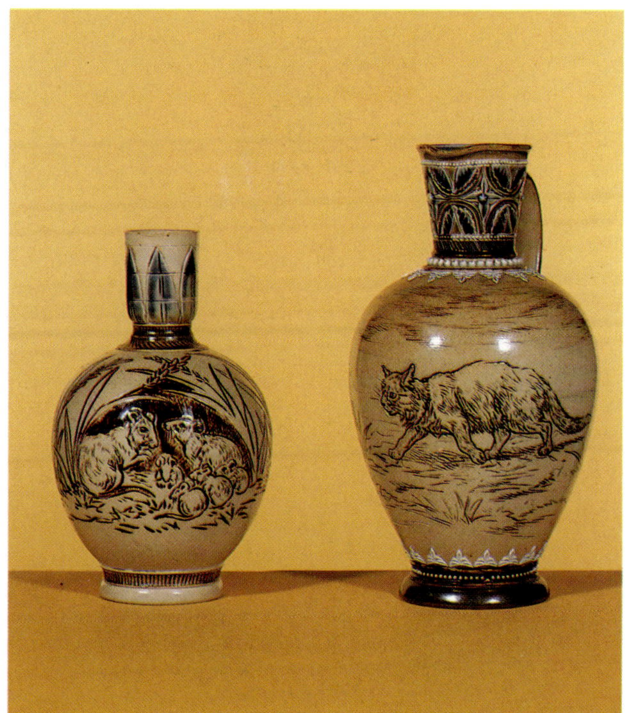

21. *Jug with a family of mice sheltering under corn, 1873, 7¼ in. and jug with a cat stalking garden birds, 1878, 9in. See No. 29.*

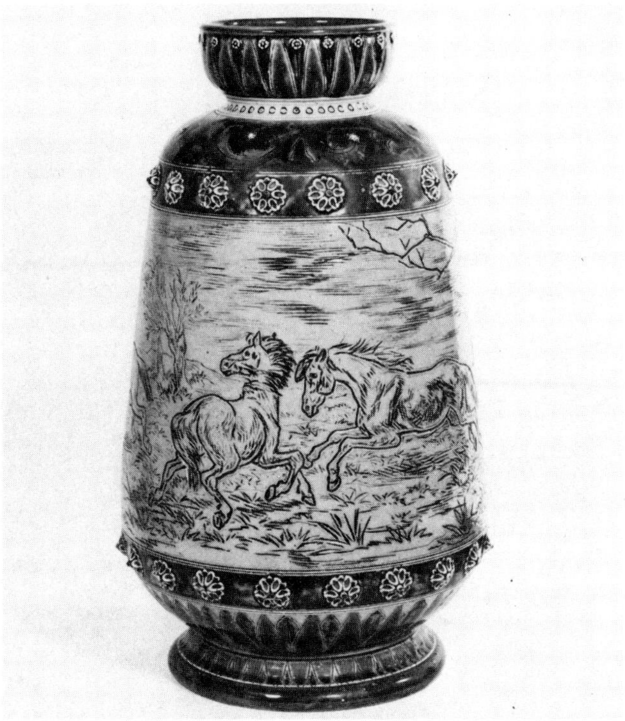

22. Vase with horses in a landscape, borders attributed to Arthur Barlow, 1875, 15¾in.

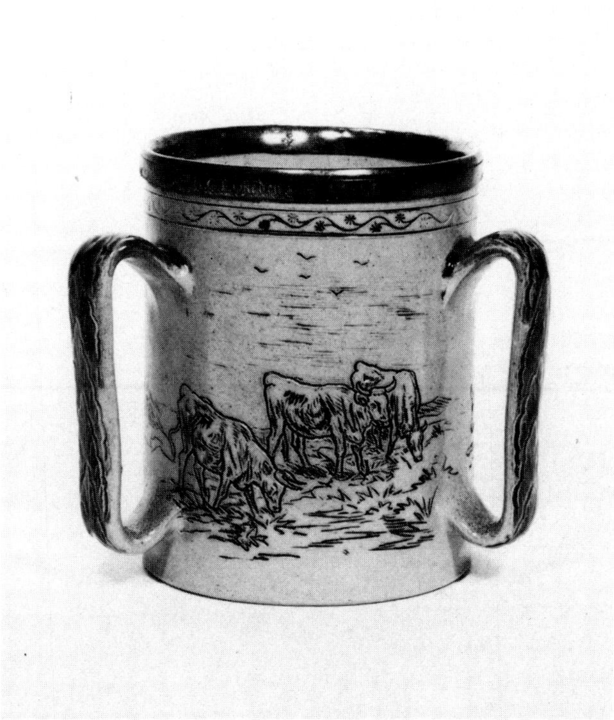

23. Three-handled loving cup with cows in pasture, 1875, 5¾in.

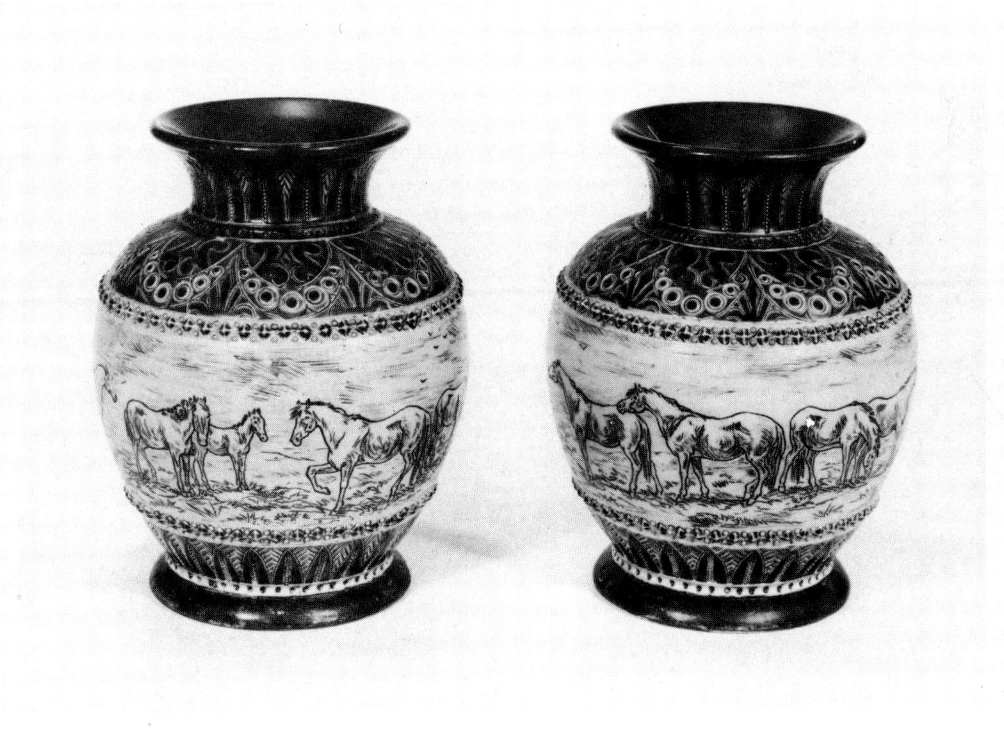

24. Pair of vases each with a continuous scene of horses in a landscape, borders by Frank Butler, 1877, 9¼in.

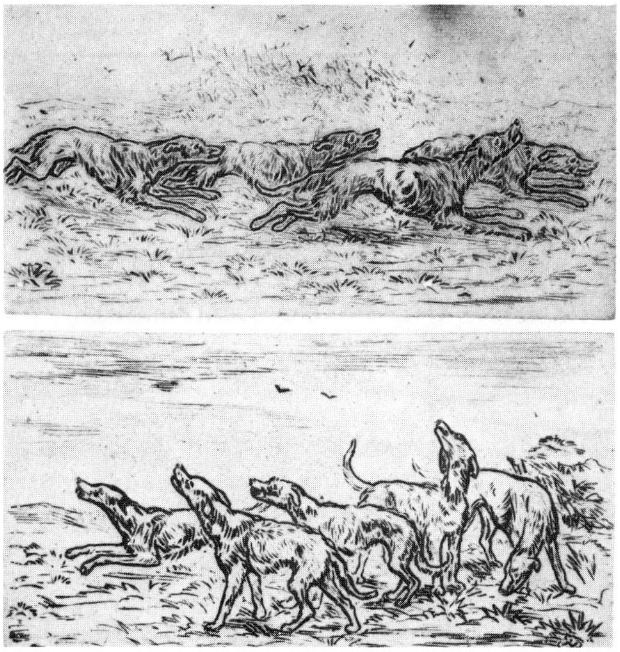

25. *Pair of plaques, probably for furniture, with dogs on the scent, c. 1875, 4¼ in. x 8¼ in.*

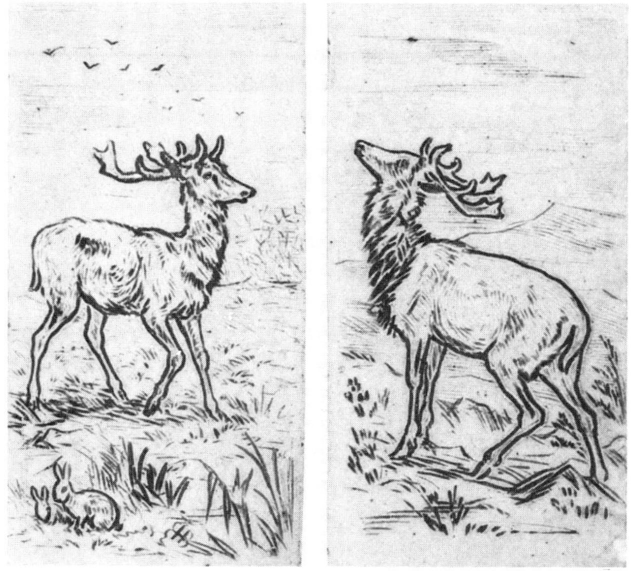

26. *Similar pair of plaques with deer in landscape, c. 1875, 6½ in. x 3¼ in.*

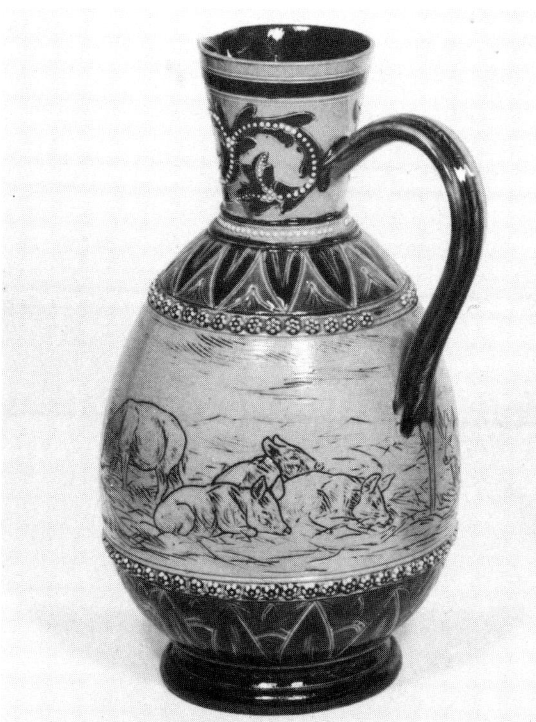

27. *Jug with young pigs rooting and sleeping, 1878, 9in.*

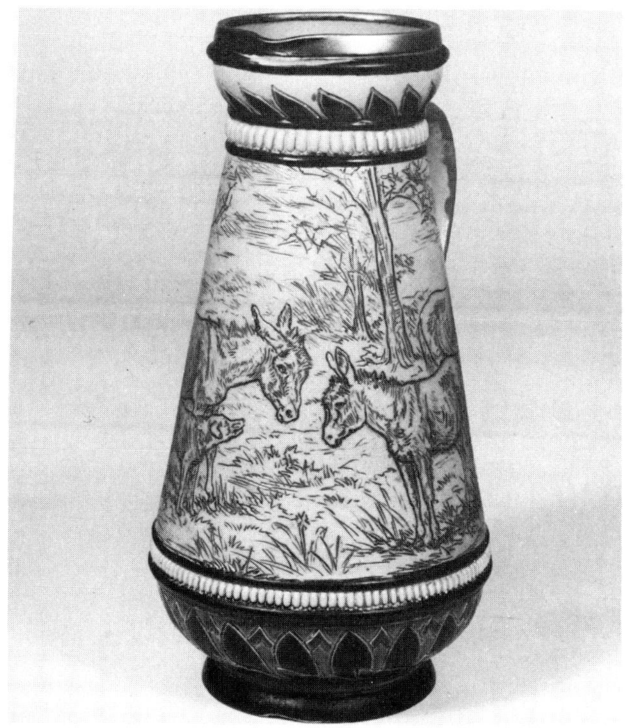

28. *Jug with donkeys, a horse, cow and dog in a wooded landscape, borders by Francis E. Lee, dated 1878, 9½ in.*

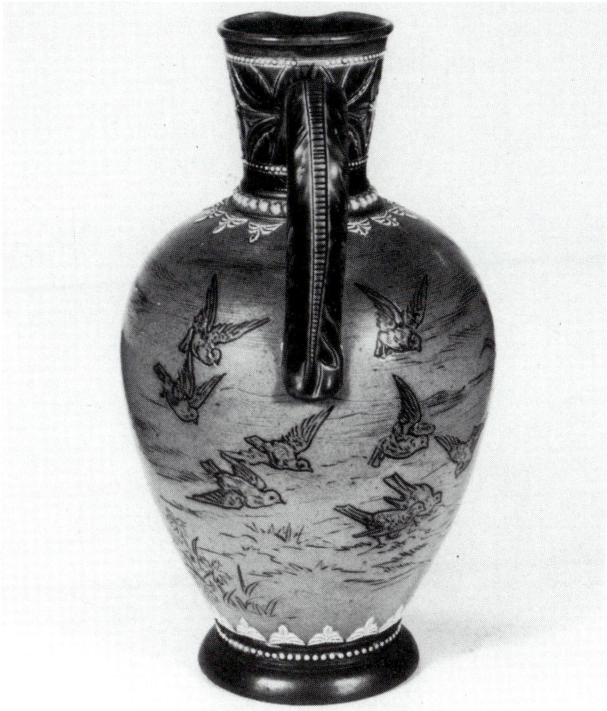

29. Jug with a cat stalking garden birds, 1878, 9in.

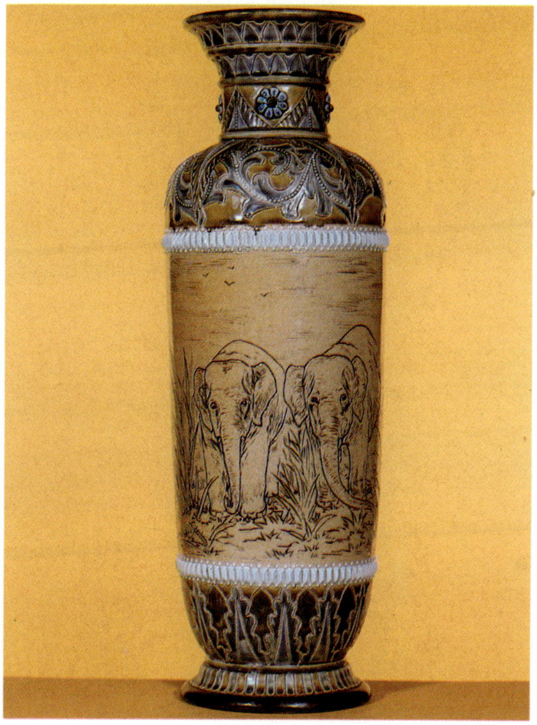

30. Rare vase with a panel of elephants and another with sleeping lions, borders by Emily Stormer, 1877, 16¾in.

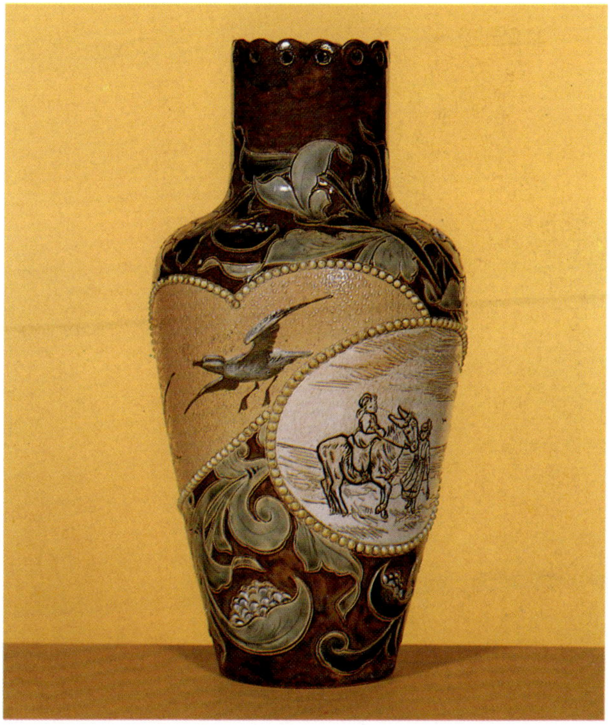

31. Vase, panel of birds in flight by Florence Barlow, panel by Hannah Barlow incised with children and a donkey at the seaside, foliate borders by Emily E. Stormer, c. 1885, 11in.

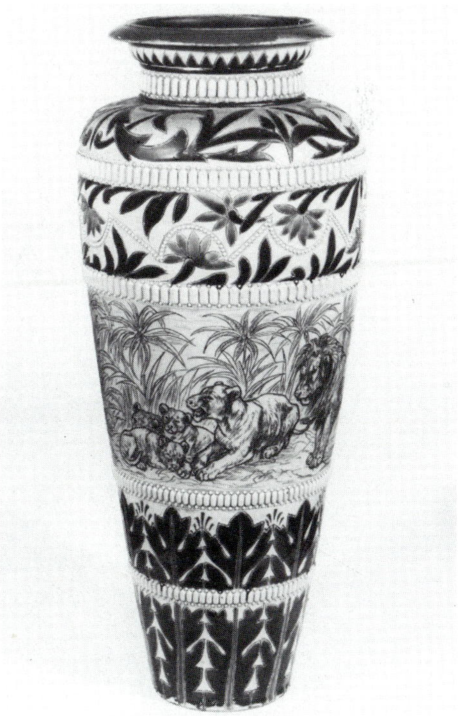

32. Vase with a pride of lions, borders by Florence Barlow, 1879, 17in.

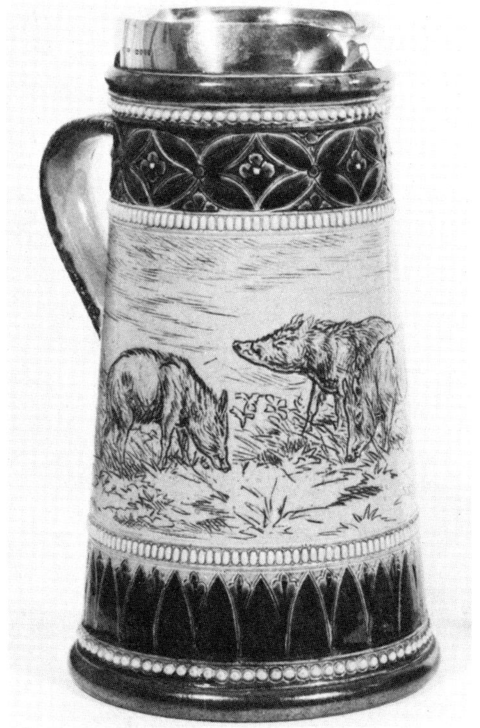

33. *Lemonade Jug with pigs, borders by Alice Budden, silver mounts, 1879, 9¼ in.*

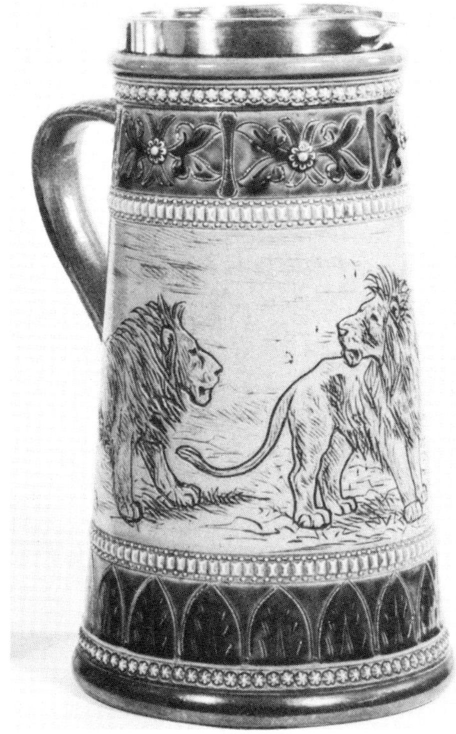

34. *Lemonade Jug with lions, borders attributed to Constance Redford, silver mounts, 1880, 9½ in.*

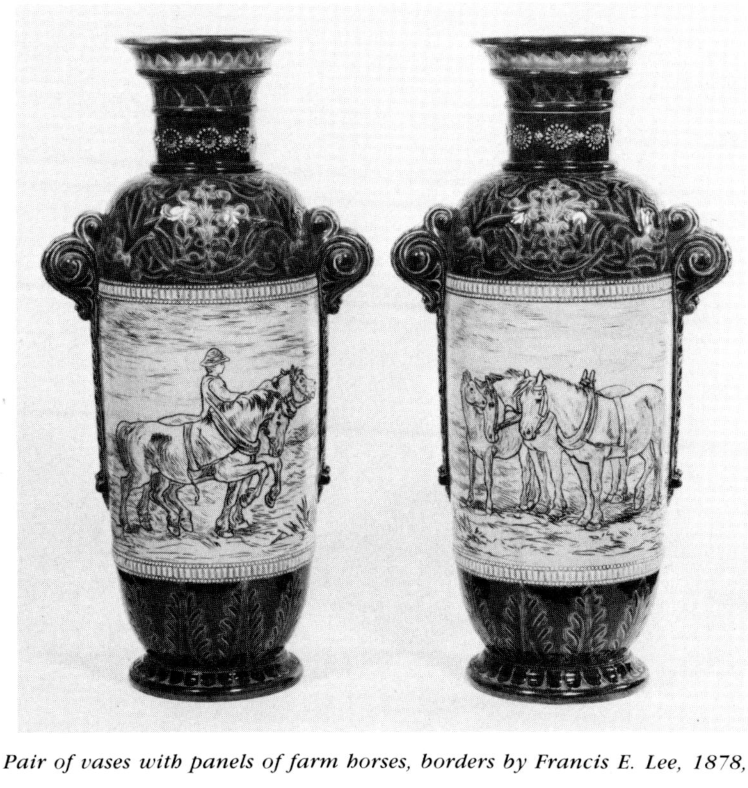

35. *Pair of vases with panels of farm horses, borders by Francis E. Lee, 1878, 16½ in.*

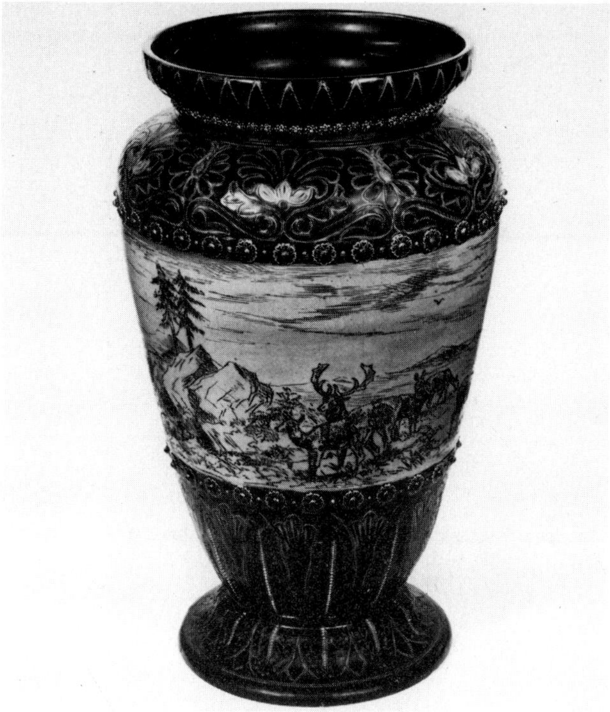

36. Pair of vases, one with a fox challenging a herd of deer, the other with deer, borders by Frances E. Lee, 1879, 15¾in.

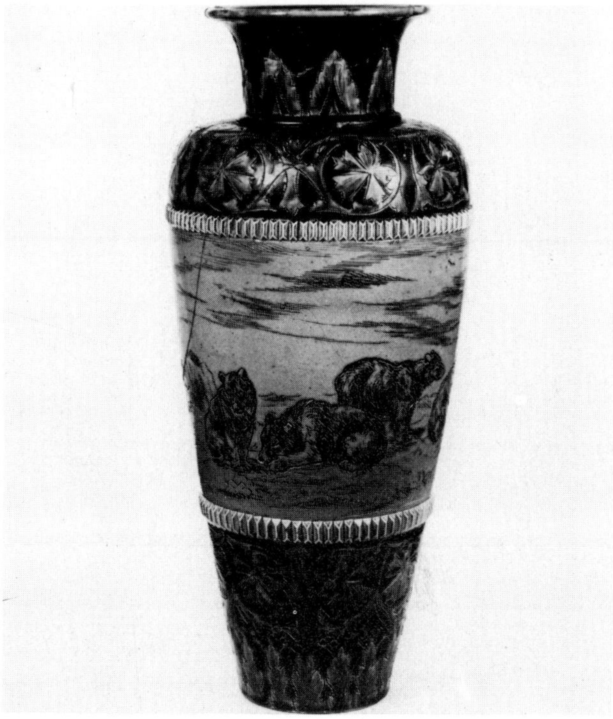

37. Vase with brown bears, borders by Elizabeth M. Small, 1880, 18in.

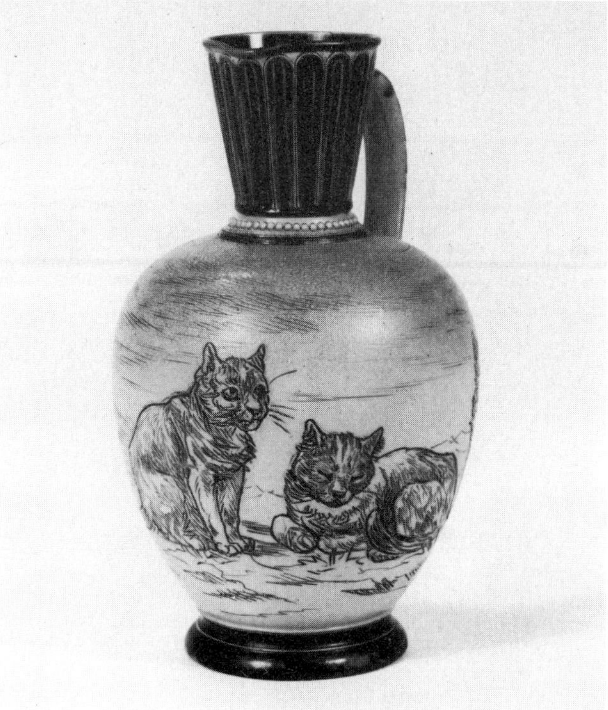

38. Jug with four cats in feline poses, 1880, 8½in.

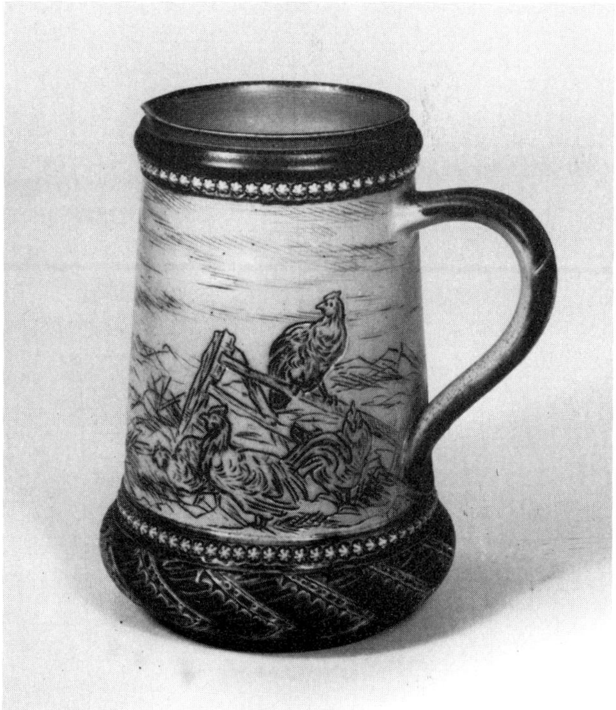

39. Jug with poultry and a donkey, borders by Alice M. Ritchin, dated 1880, 6¾in.

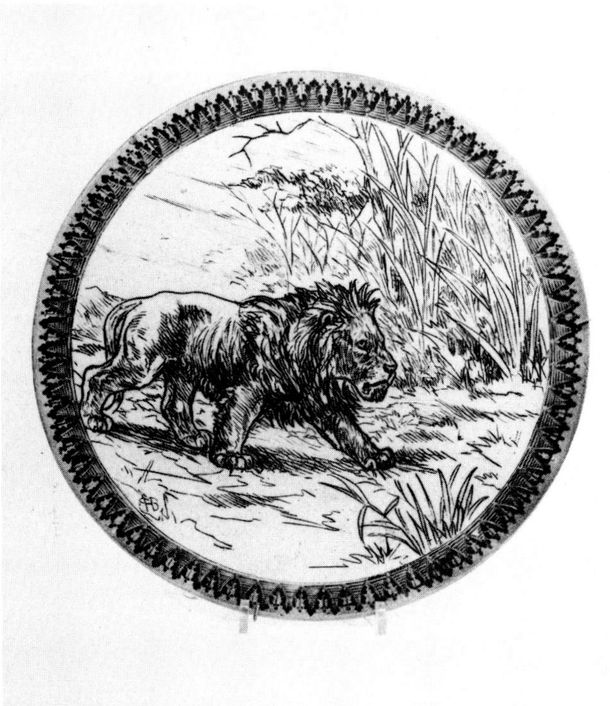

40. *Plaque with a lion, borders by Harriett L. Hibbut, 1880, 12¼ in. diam.*

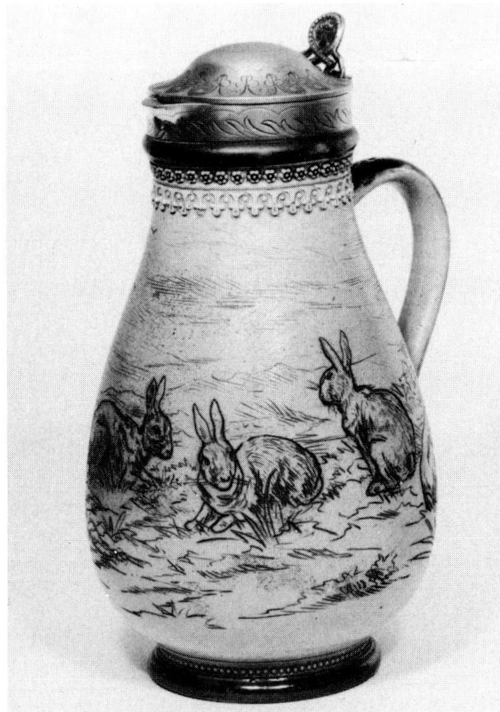

41. *Jug with plated mounts and a continuous scene of rabbits in a landscape, 1880, 9¾ in.*

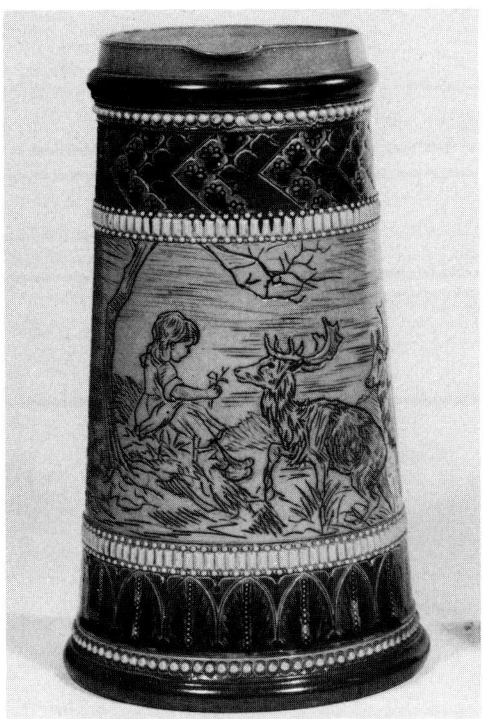

42. *Lemonade Jug with a little girl and tame deer, borders by Nellie Garbatt, 1880, 9¼ in.*

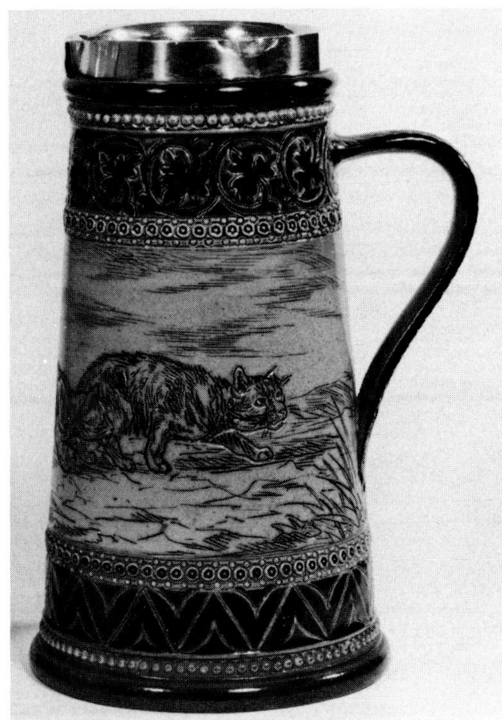

43. *Lemonade Jug with cats stalking a mouse who hides under the handle, silver mounts, 1880, 9¼ in.*

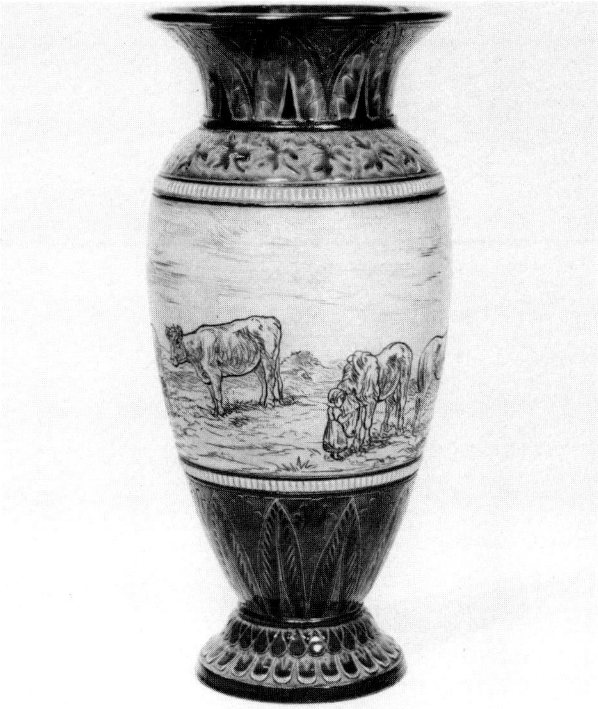

44. Vase with a little girl stroking a horse in pasture, with other horses and cattle, 1881, 15¼in.

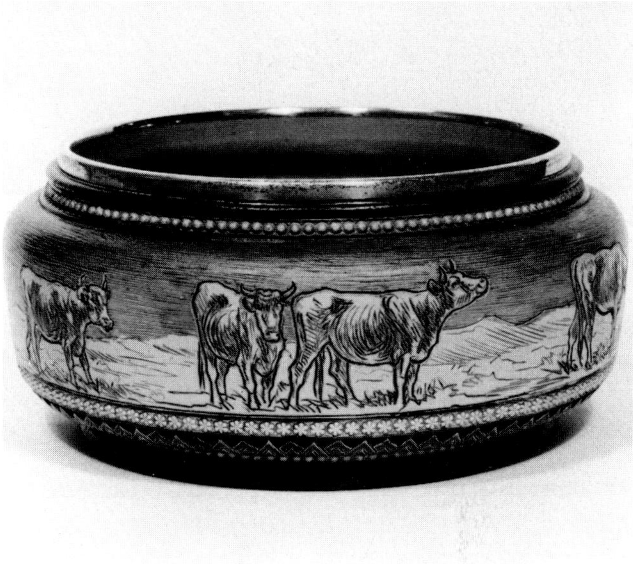

45. Bowl with plated mount and a frieze of cows, borders by Louisa Wakely, 1881, 9in. diam.

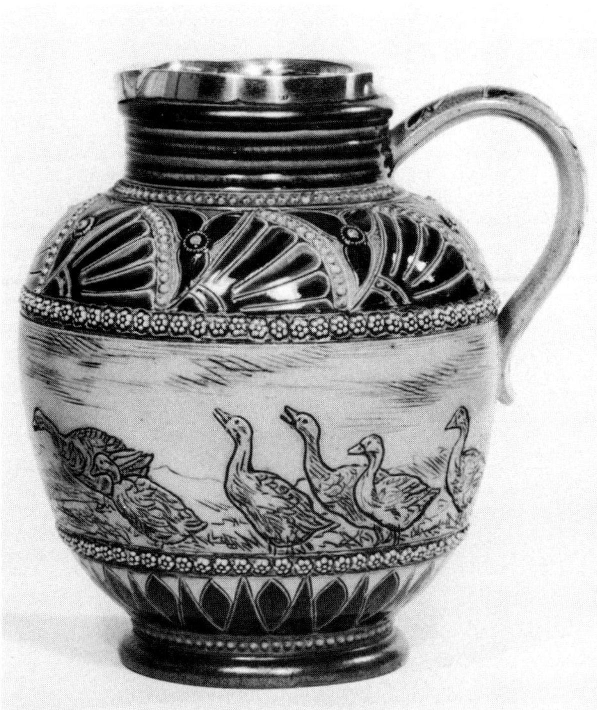

46. Silver mounted jug with frieze of ducks approaching a recumbent dog, borders by Alice Budden, 1881, 7in.

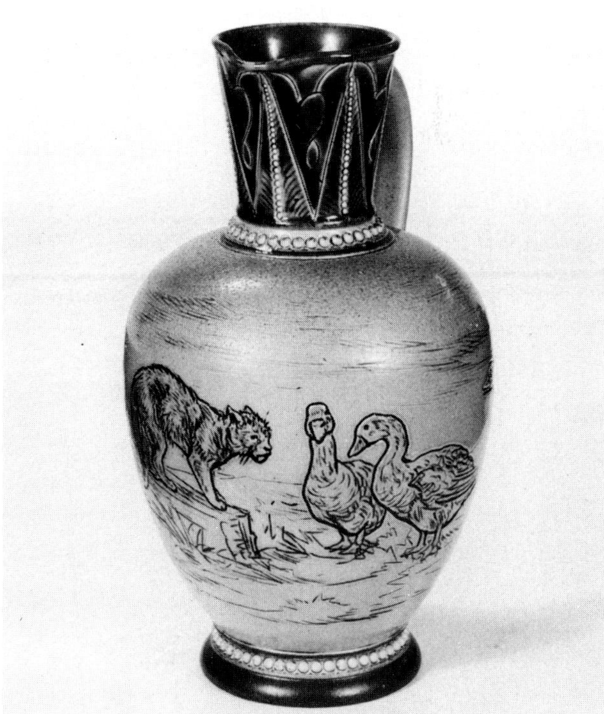

47. Jug with a cat confronting a gaggle of geese, 1881, 8½in.

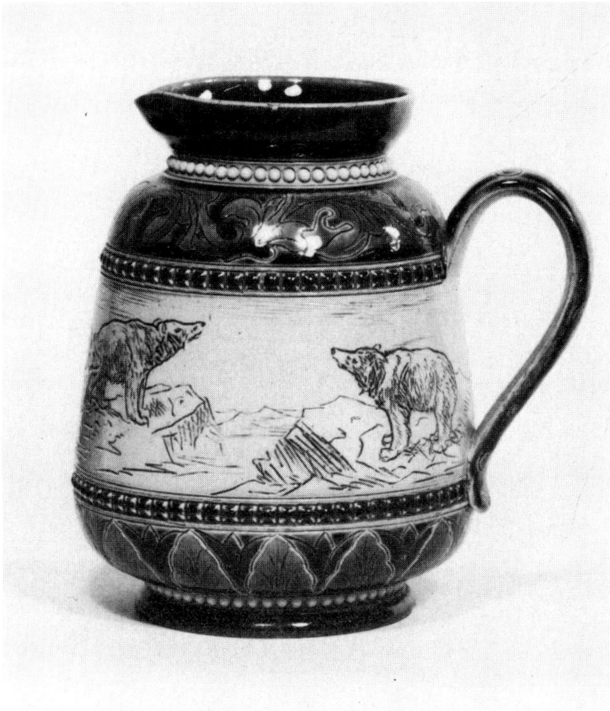

48. Jug with a band of polar bears, borders by Lucy Barlow, 1882, 6½ in.

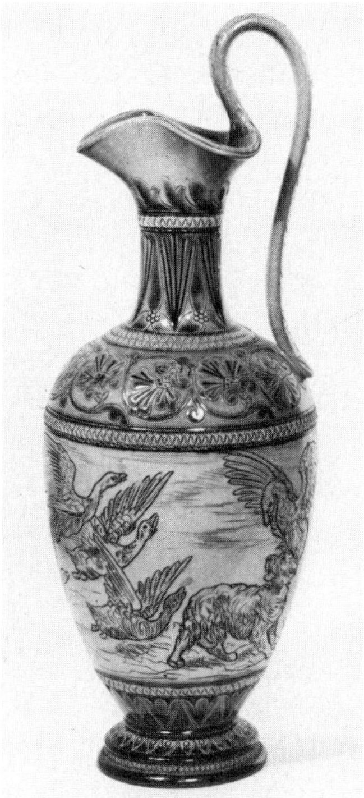

49. Ewer with a flock of geese attacking a dog, borders by Rosina Brown, 1882, 14¼ in.

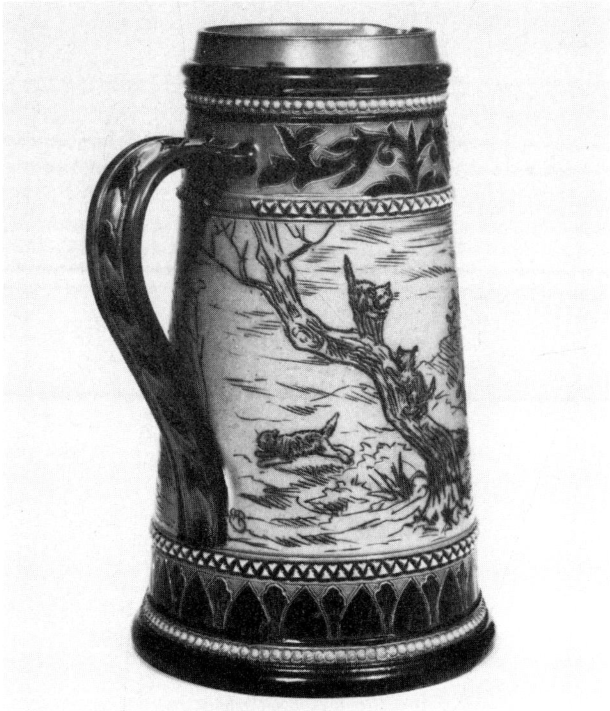

50. Lemonade Jug with a dog growling at a bristling cat defending its kittens on a tree, borders by Lucy Barlow, 1883, 9¼ in.

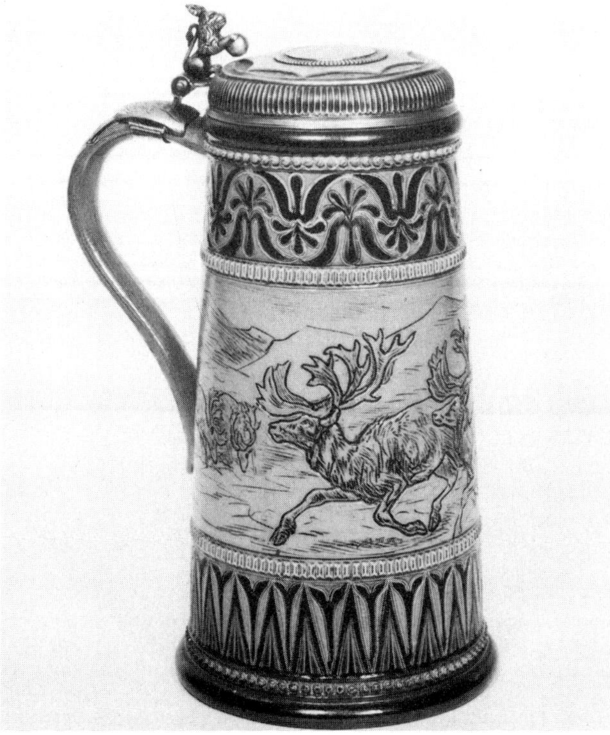

51. Tankard with antique German silver mount and running stags, borders by Alice Budden, 1882, 12in.

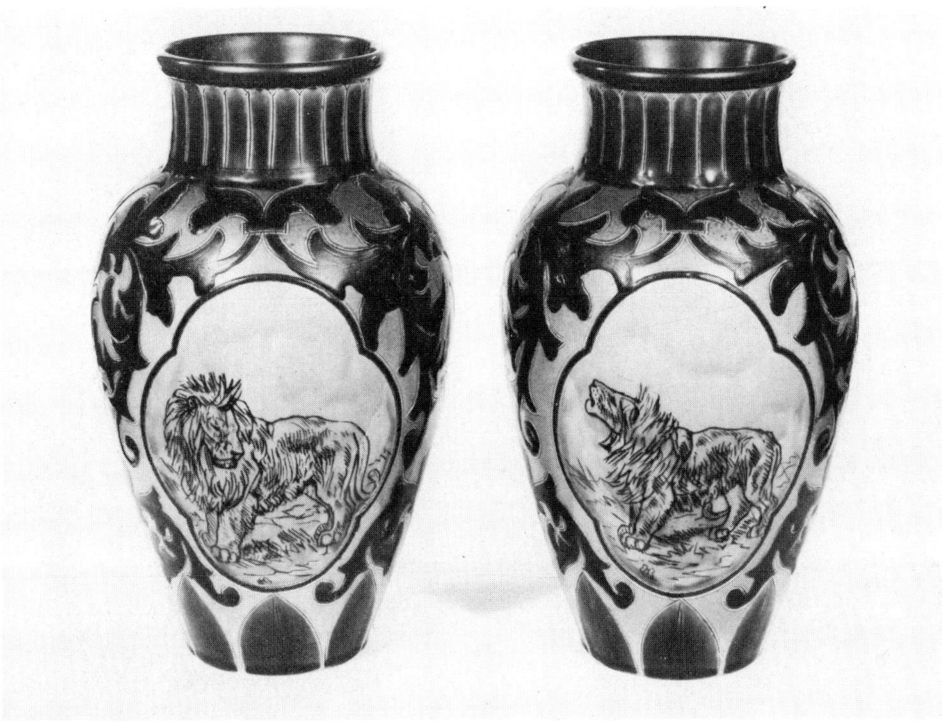

52. *Pair of vases each with two panels of lions incised and filled with a green glaze, borders by Lucy Barlow, 1884, 11¾in.*

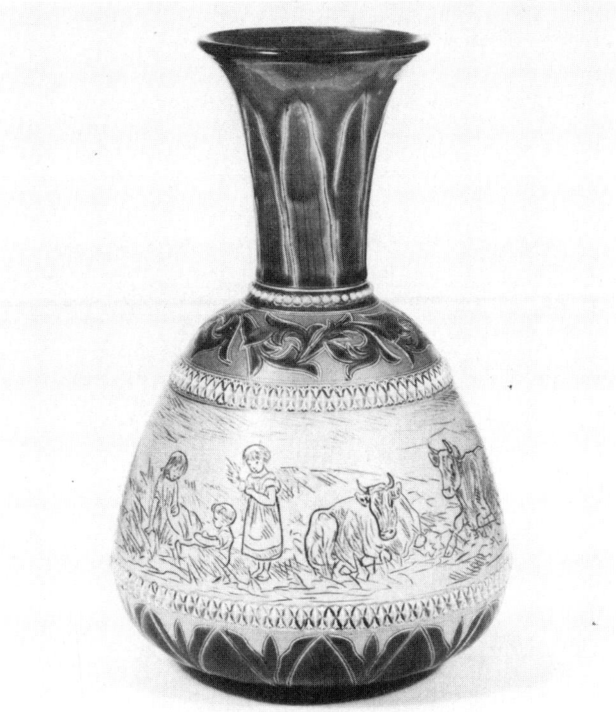

53. *Vase with children playing in a field with grazing cows, borders by Lucy Barlow, 1884, 9½in.*

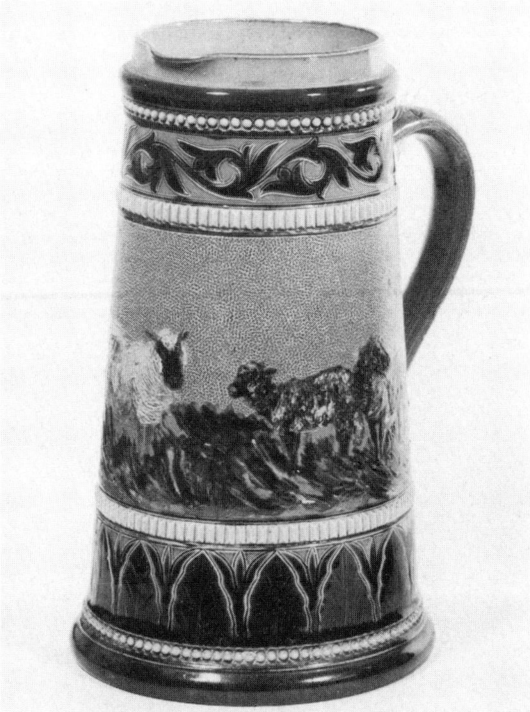

54. *Lemonade jug painted with pâte-sur-pâte sheep, borders by Lucy Barlow, 1884, 9¼in.*

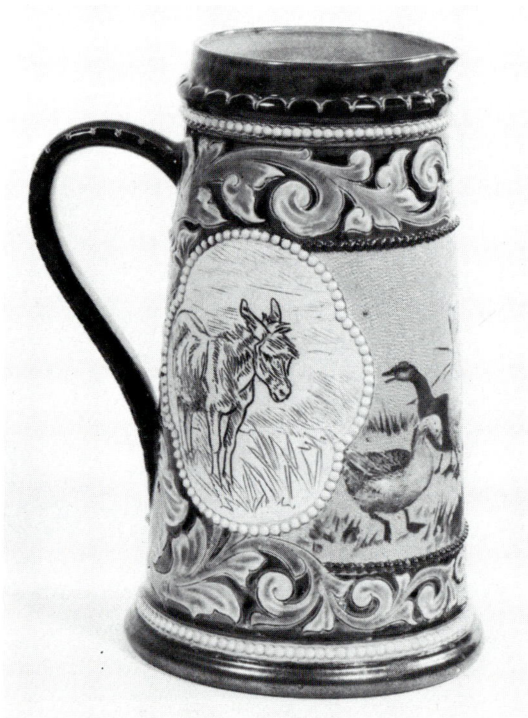

55. Lemonade jug painted with pâte-sur-pâte geese by Florence Barlow and panels with a pony and donkey by Hannah Barlow, borders by Emily E. Stormer, c. 1885, 9in.

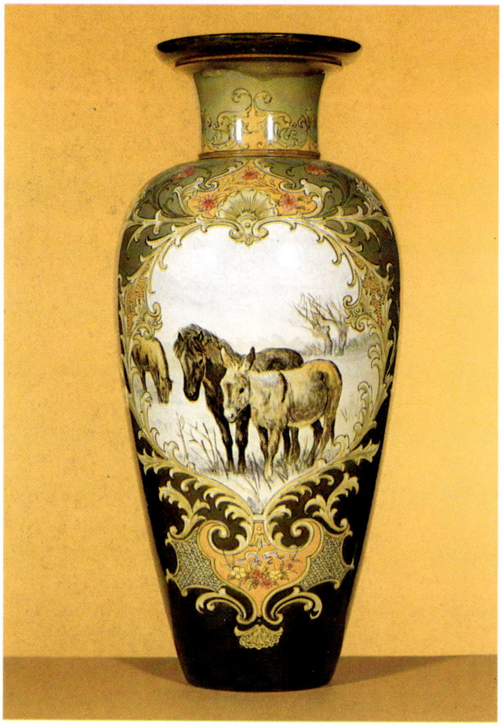

56. Faience vase painted with horses and a donkey in a winter landscape, scrolls and flowers by Katie Blake Smallfield, c. 1885, 17½in.

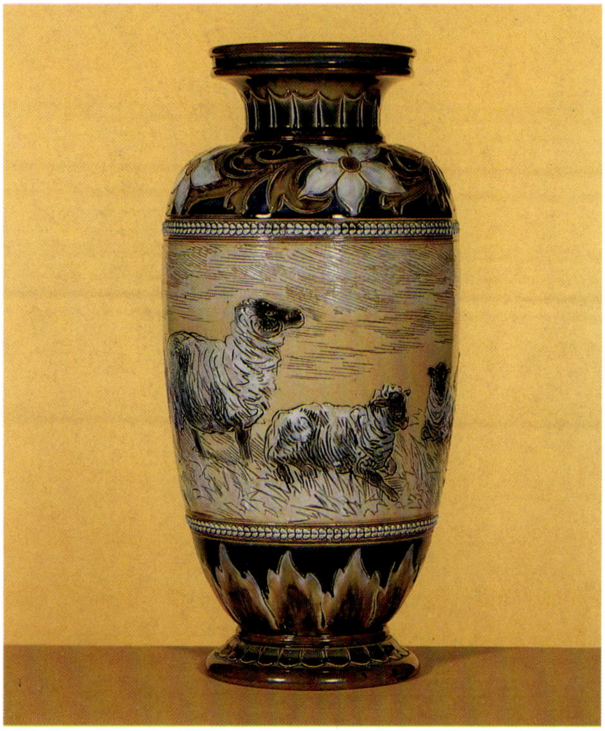

57. Vase with pâte-sur-pâte sheep, borders by Eliza Simmance, c. 1895, 12in.

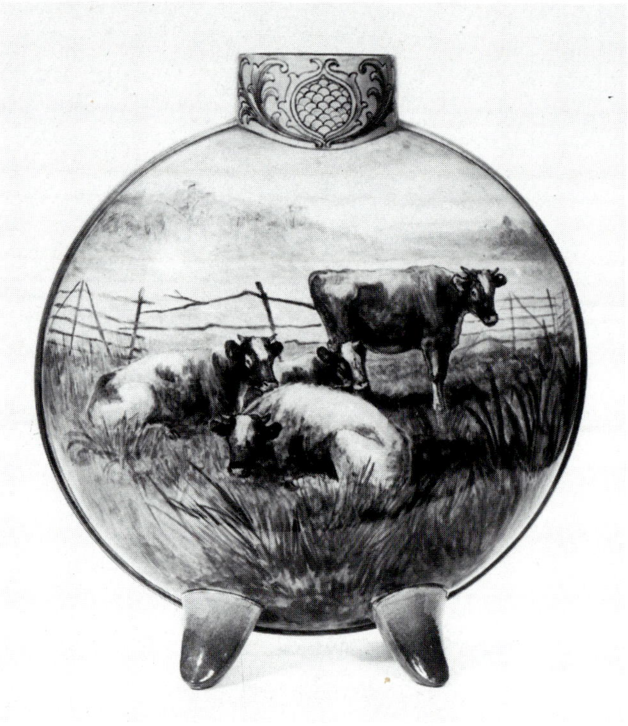

58. Faience moon flask painted with cows in a field, borders by Katie Blake Smithfield, c. 1885, 14in.

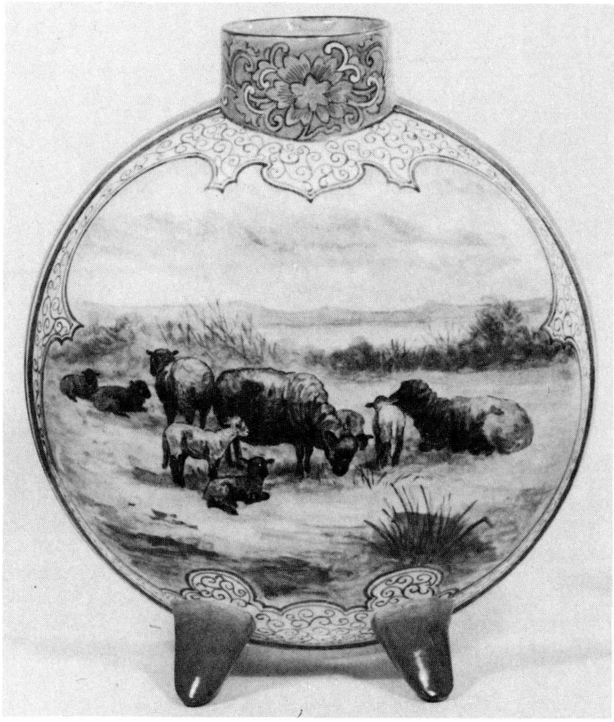

59. Flattened, circular, faience vase painted with sheep and lambs in a winter landscape, borders by Katie Blake Smallfield, c. 1885, 9½in.

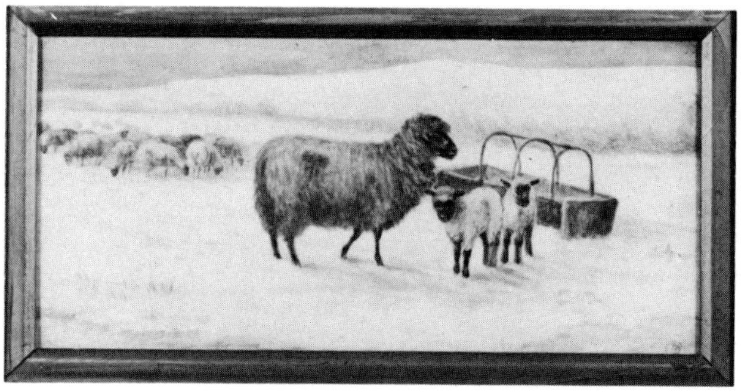

60. Faience plaque painted with sheep feeding in the snow, c. 1890, length 10in.

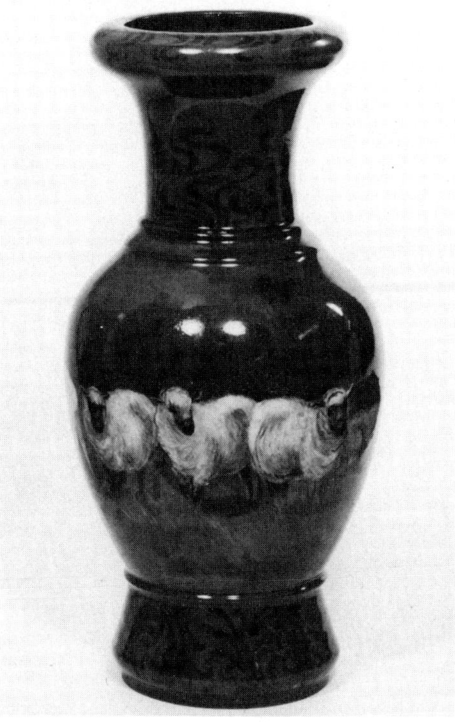

61. Faience vase painted with sheep, borders by Katie Blake Smallfield, c. 1885, 9¾in.

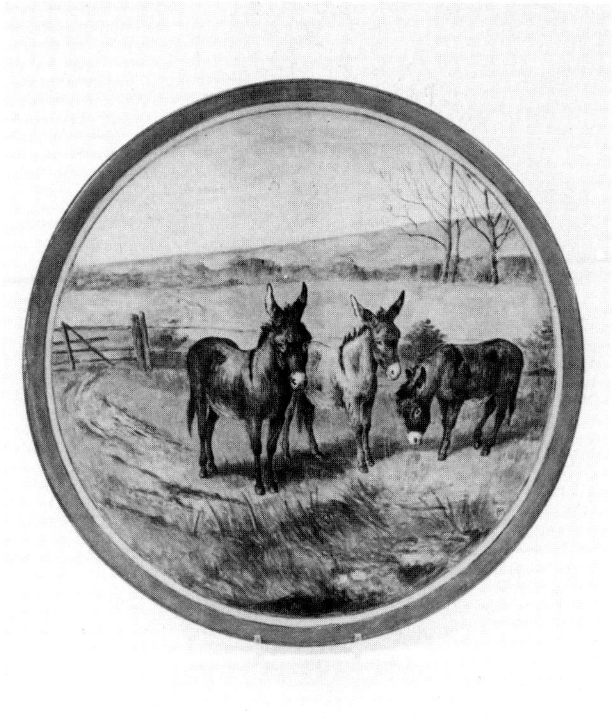

62. Faience plaque painted with donkeys in pasture, c. 1895, 17½in. diam.

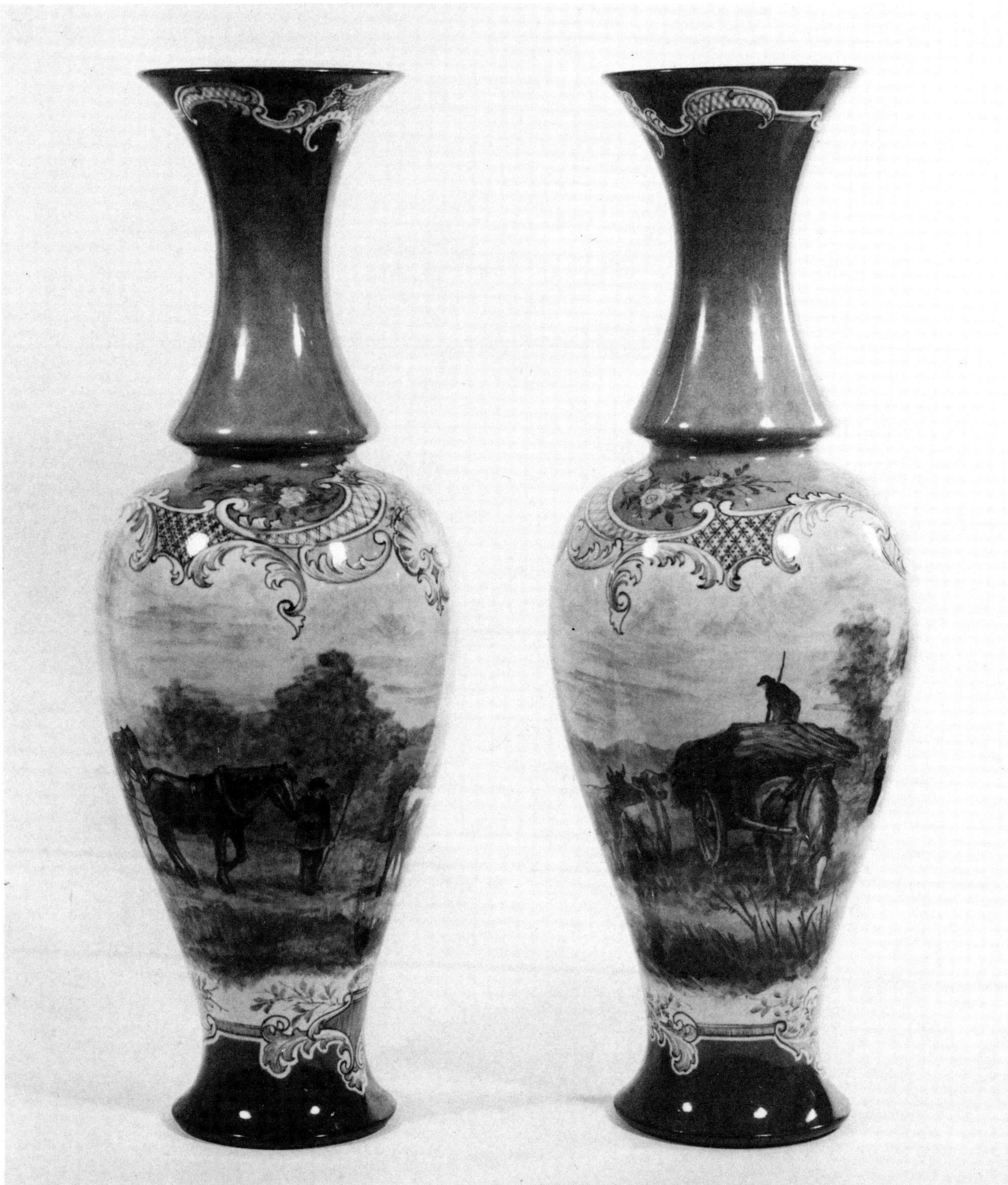

63. Pair of faience vases with panels of cattle and carts of hay, borders by Katie Blake Smallfield and Josephine Durtnall, c. 1895, 17½ in.

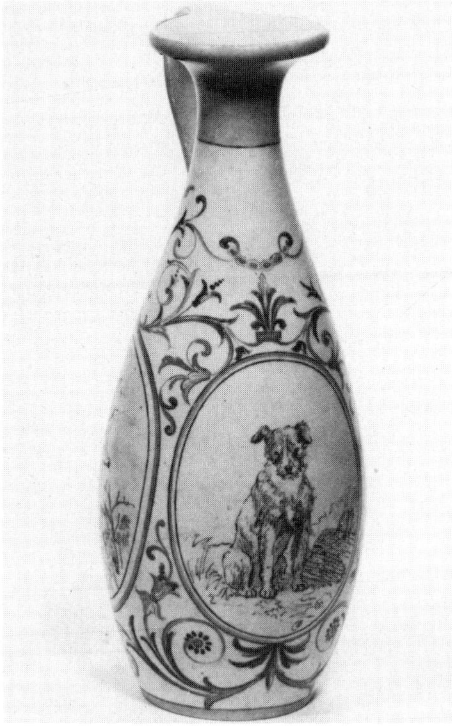

64. Carrara ware ewer painted with a dog, donkey and a stag, scrolls by Mary Denley, c. 1885, 8in.

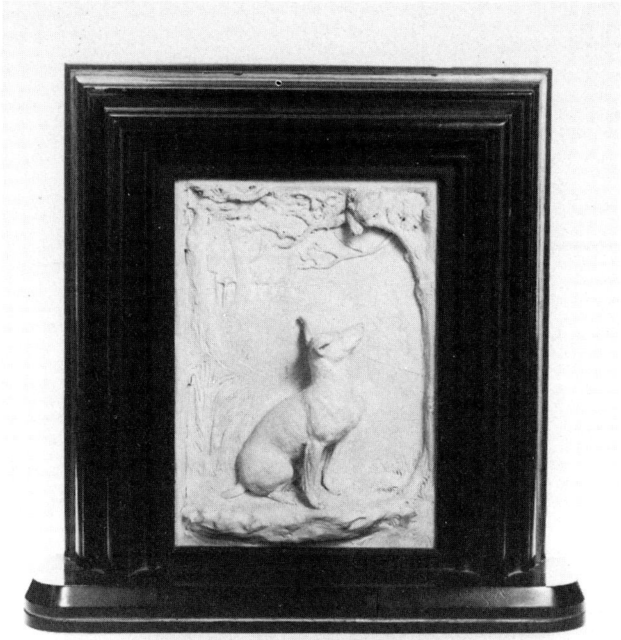

65. Terracotta plaque titled "So near and yet so far", the animals modelled in high relief, 1890, 10in. x 7in. Exhibited at Royal Academy in 1890.

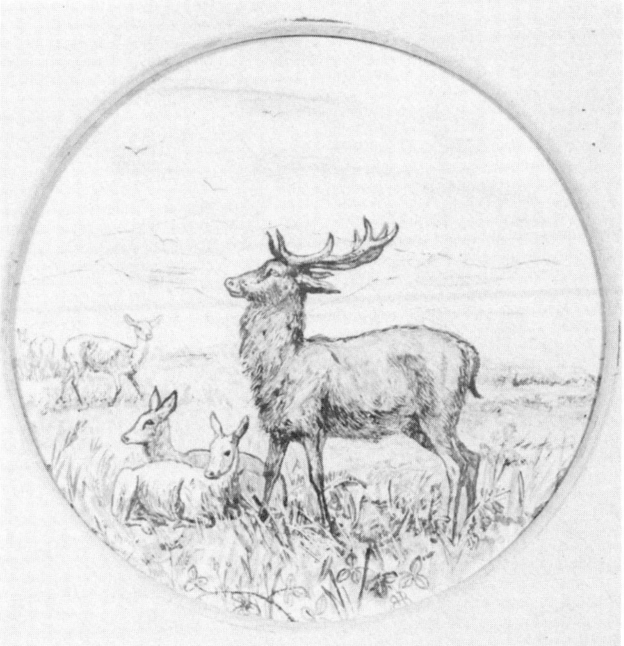

66. Circular porcelain plaque painted with deer by Hannah Barlow, c. 1890, 7¾in. diam.

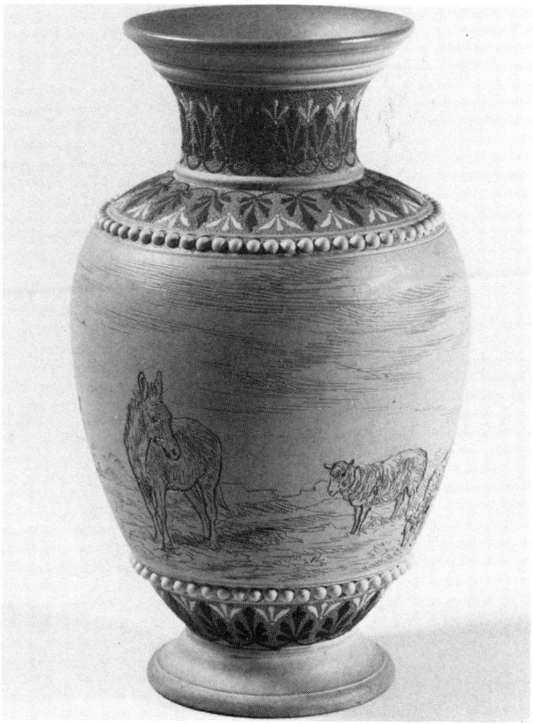

67. Silicon vase with sheep and donkeys, 1882, 8¾in.

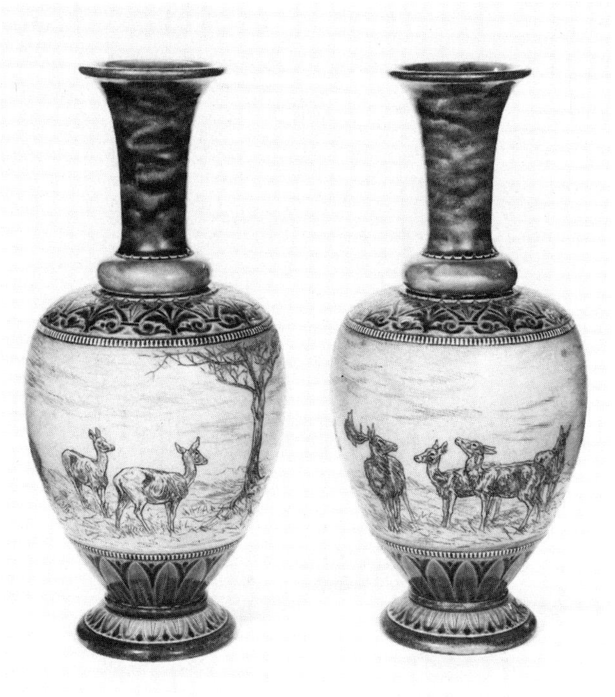

68. Pair of vases with continuous scenes of deer in landscapes, borders by Emily Welch, 1885, 21¾ in.

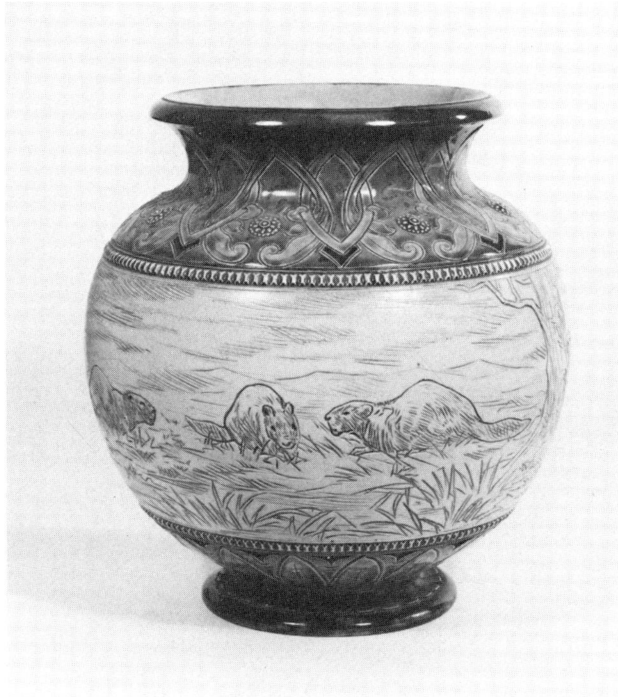

69. Vase with beavers, borders by Emily Stormer, 1886, 9¾ in.

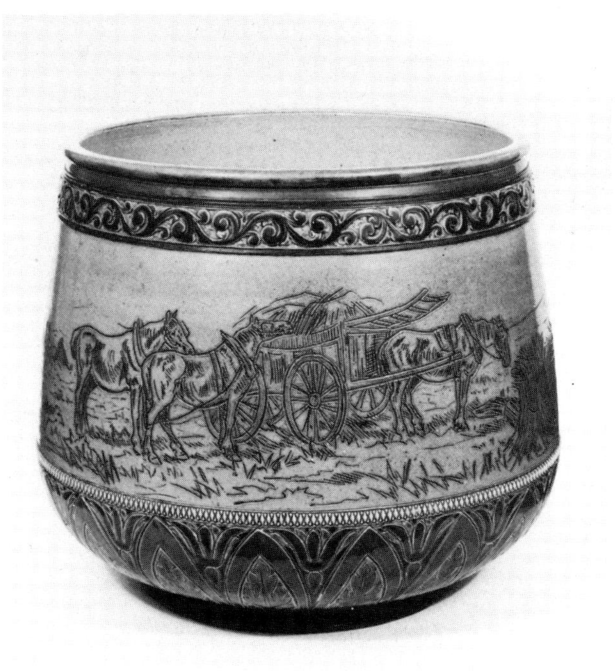

70. Jardiniere with horses, cows and farmworkers in a harvesting scene, borders by A.B., c. 1885, 12¼ in.

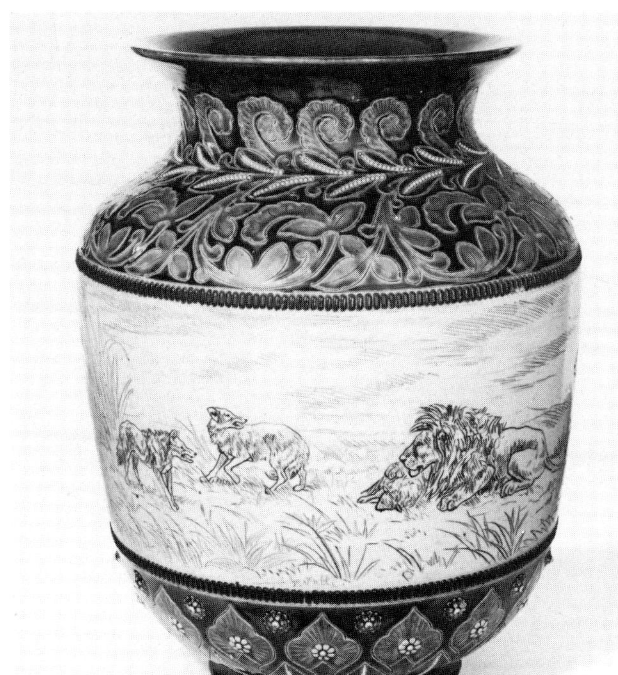

71. Vase with two wolves contesting a sheep, the kill of two lions, inscribed 'Ye Fable', 1885, 21½ in.

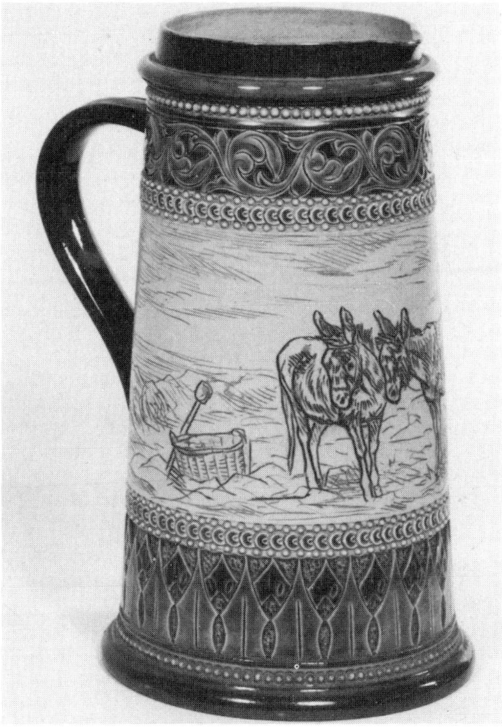

72. *Lemonade Jug with donkeys by the seaside, 1887, 9¼ in.*

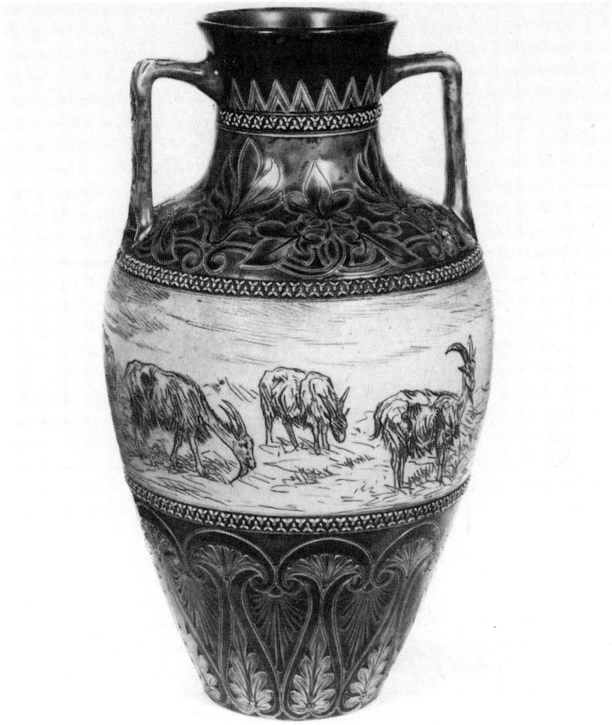

73. *Vase with a continuous scene of goats in mountain pasture, borders by Alice Budden, 1886, 14½ in.*

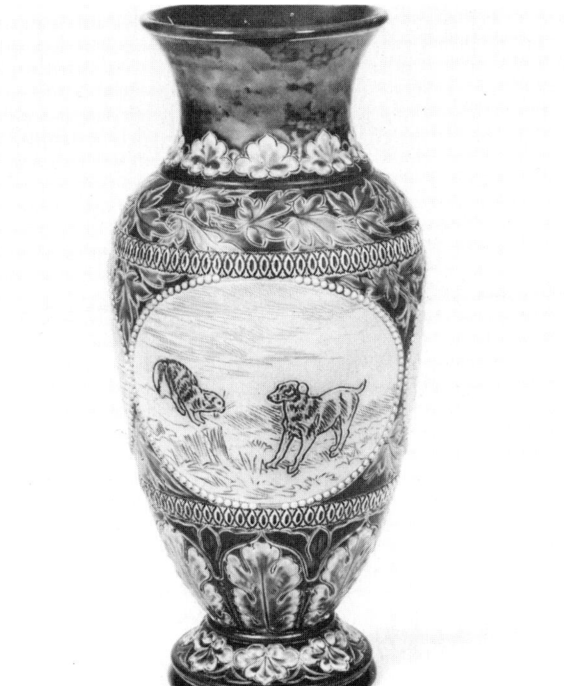

74. *Vase with three panels illustrating the sequence of a dog chasing a cat up a tree, borders by A.B., c. 1888, 12¾ in.*

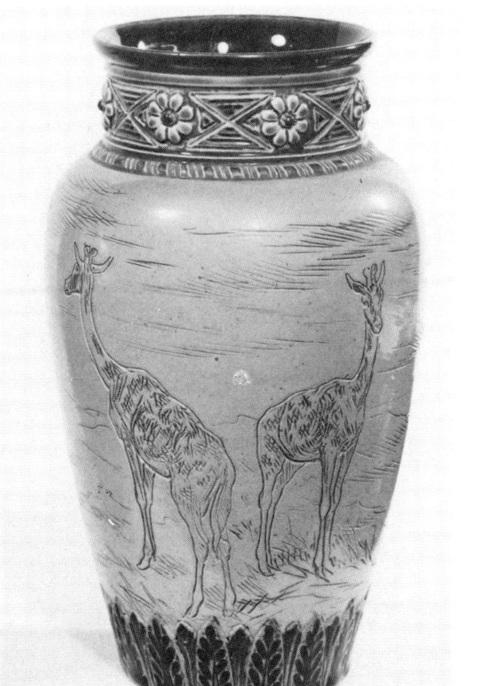

75. *Vase with giraffes, borders by A.B., c. 1888, 10in.*

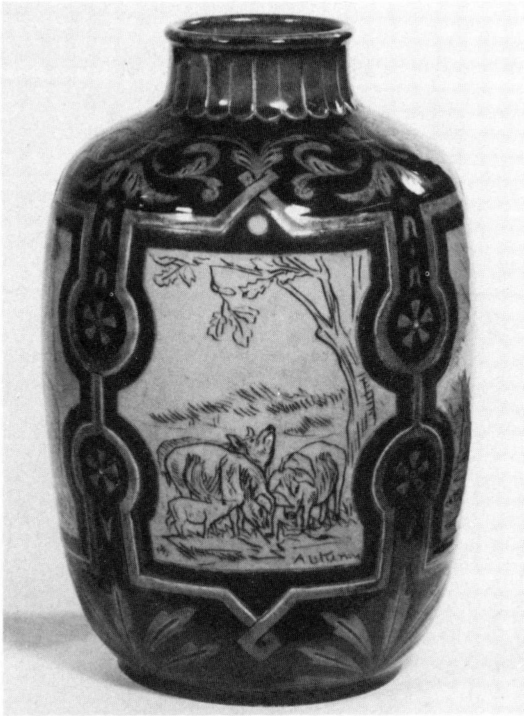

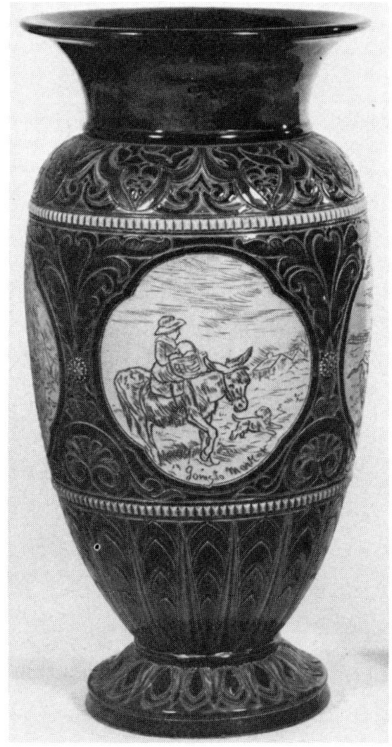

76. *Vase form (without a base) incised and filled with a green glaze, showing four panels of the seasons, borders by Lucy Barlow and Eliza Simmance, c. 1885, 10¾in.*

77. *Vase with four scenes, 'summertime' with cows, 'going to market' on a donkey, 'calves' and 'friends', a pair of donkeys, borders by A.B., 1888, 14½in.*

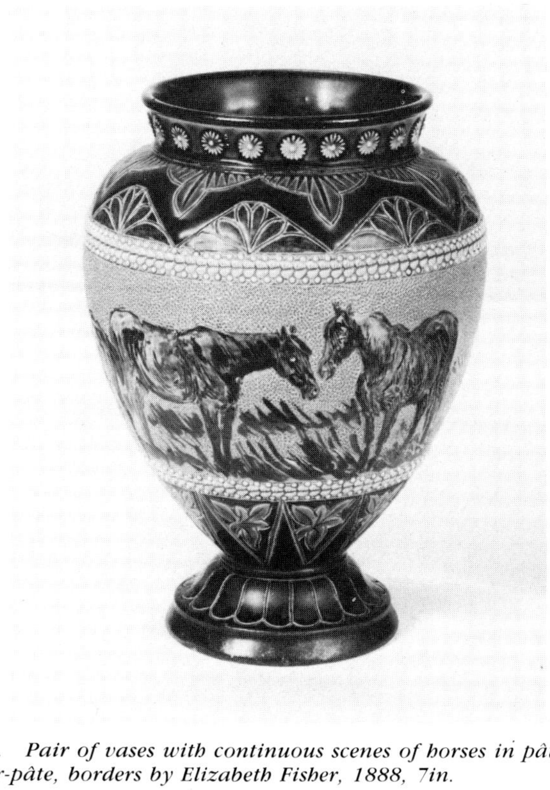

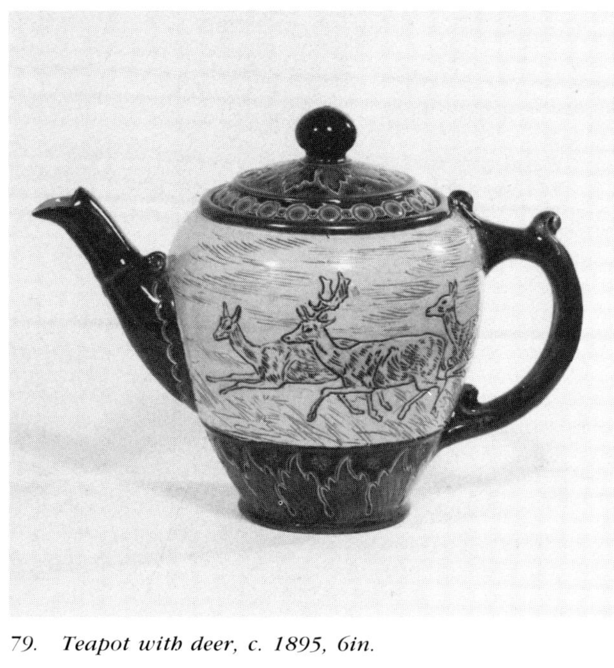

78. *Pair of vases with continuous scenes of horses in pâte-sur-pâte, borders by Elizabeth Fisher, 1888, 7in.*

79. *Teapot with deer, c. 1895, 6in.*

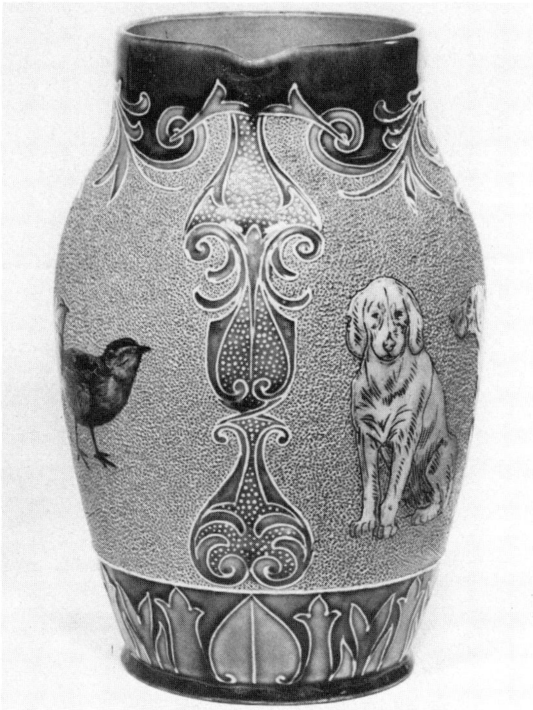

80. Jug painted with pâte-sur-pâte with chicks by Florence Barlow, incised and glazed with two hounds by Hannah Barlow, c. 1895, 9½in.

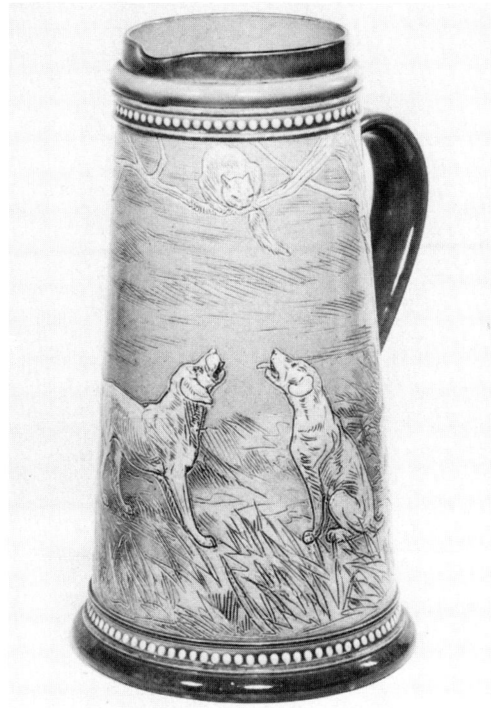

81. Lemonade Jug with dogs tormenting a cat in a tree, c. 1895, 9¼in.

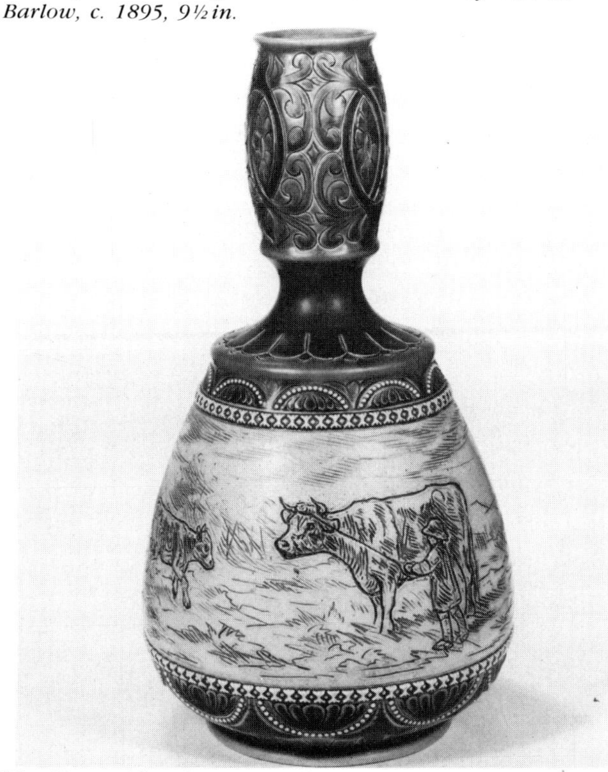

82. Vase with a farm scene, borders by A.B., c. 1895, 11½in.

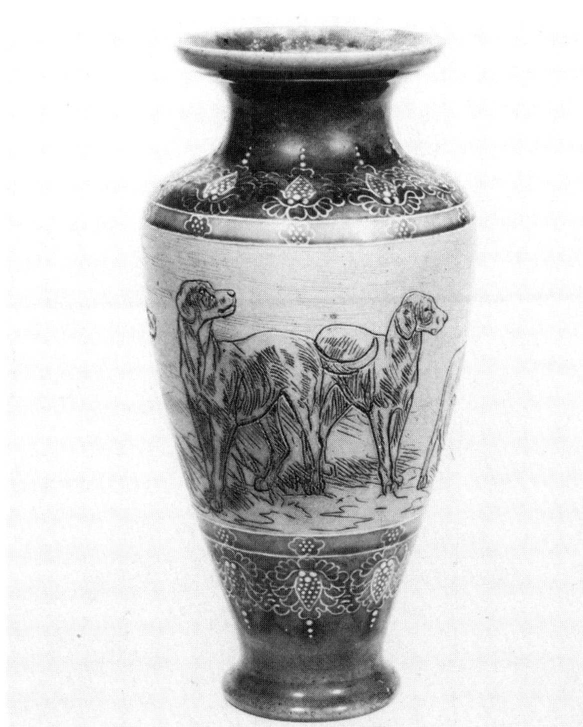

83. Vase with frieze of fox hounds, borders by Florence Roberts, c. 1895, 12in.

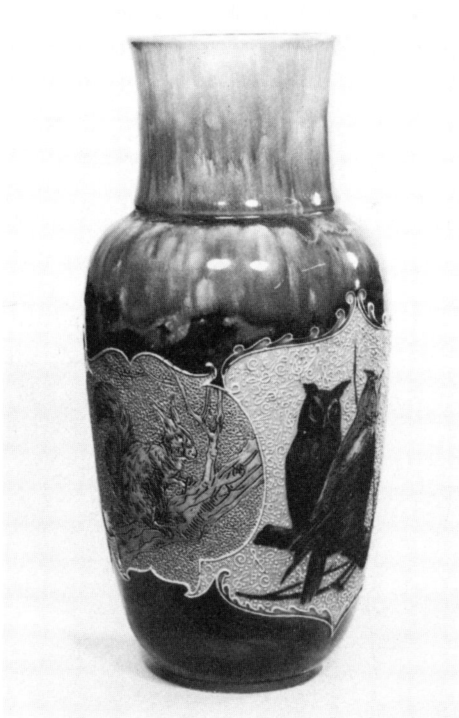

84. *Vase painted with owls in pâte-sur-pâte by Florence Barlow and incised with squirrels by Hannah Barlow on shaped panels, c. 1895, 12¼ in.*

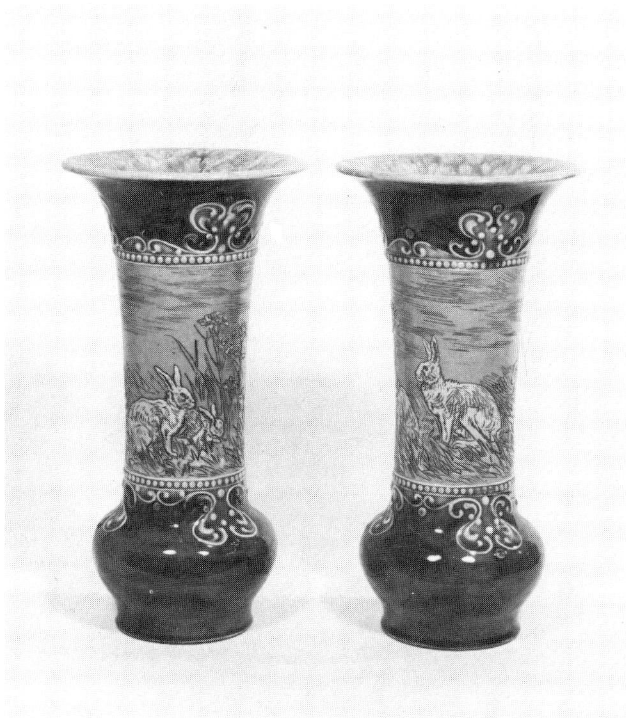

85. *Pair of Vases with continuous scenes of rabbits amongst cow parsley, borders by Florence Roberts, c. 1895, 11in.*

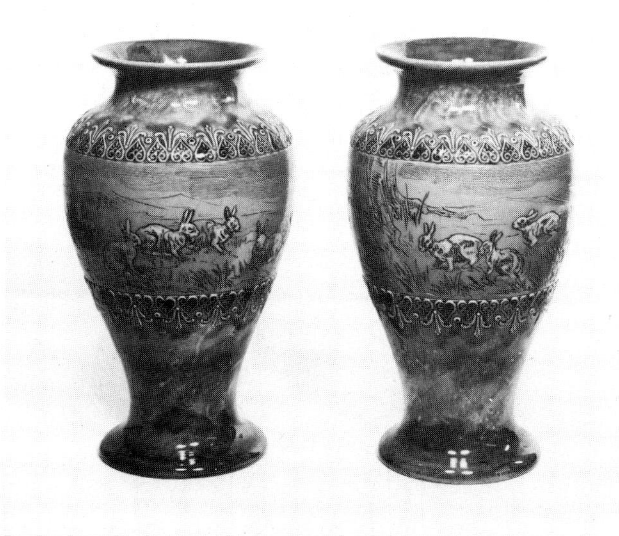

86. *Pair of vases each incised and glazed with frieze of rabbits playing beneath a tree, 1907, 10¾ in.*

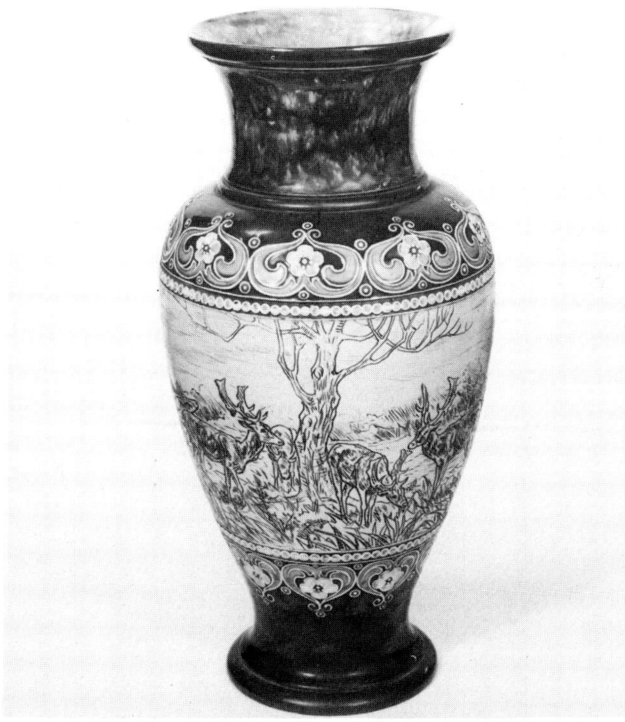

87. *Vase with a herd of deer in a wooded landscape, borders by Florence Roberts, 1903, 18½ in.*

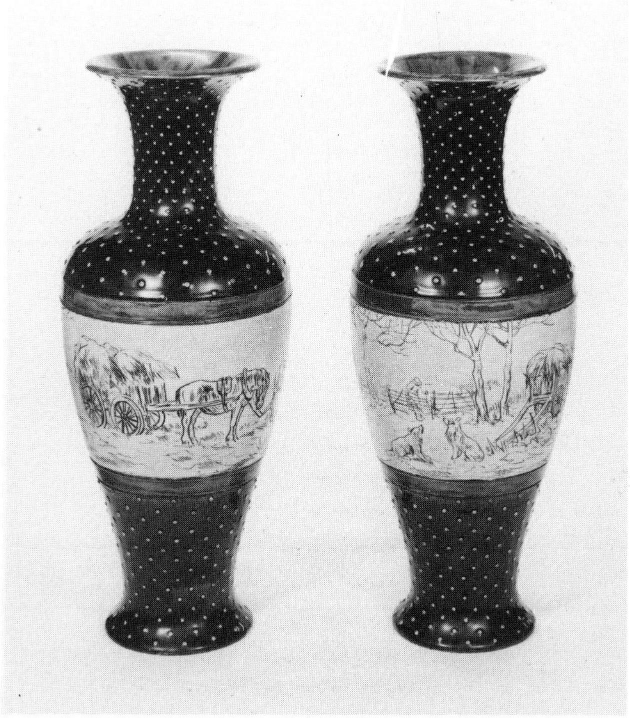

88. Pair of vases with farming scenes including horses, carts of hay, a cottage, dogs and a farmworker, 1909, 18½in.

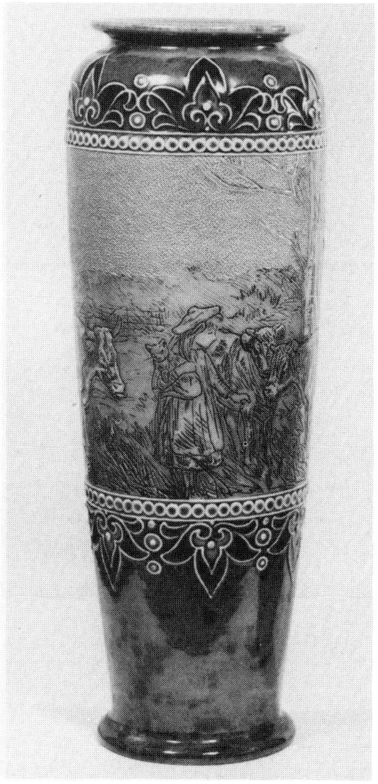

89. Vase with a young girl taking her reluctant cat to visit some cows, borders by Florence Roberts, c. 1902, 14in.

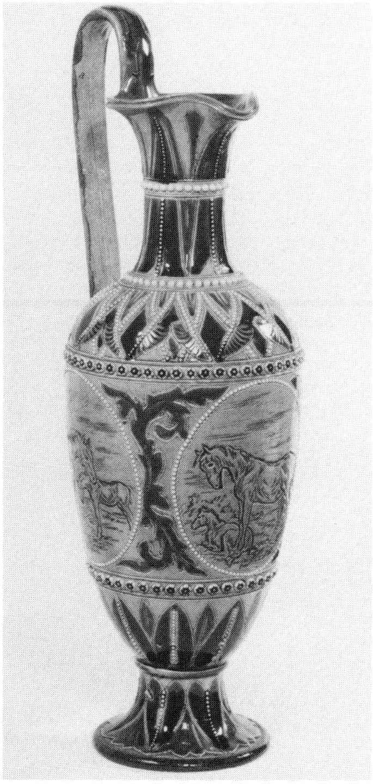

90. Ewer with panels of horses and foals by Florence Barlow, borders by Mary Aitken, 1876, 15in.

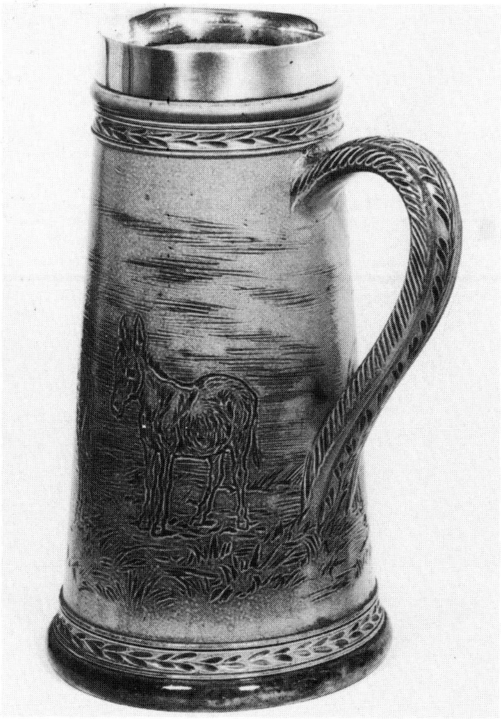

91. Lemonade Jug with horses by Florence Barlow, silver mounts, 1876, 9in.

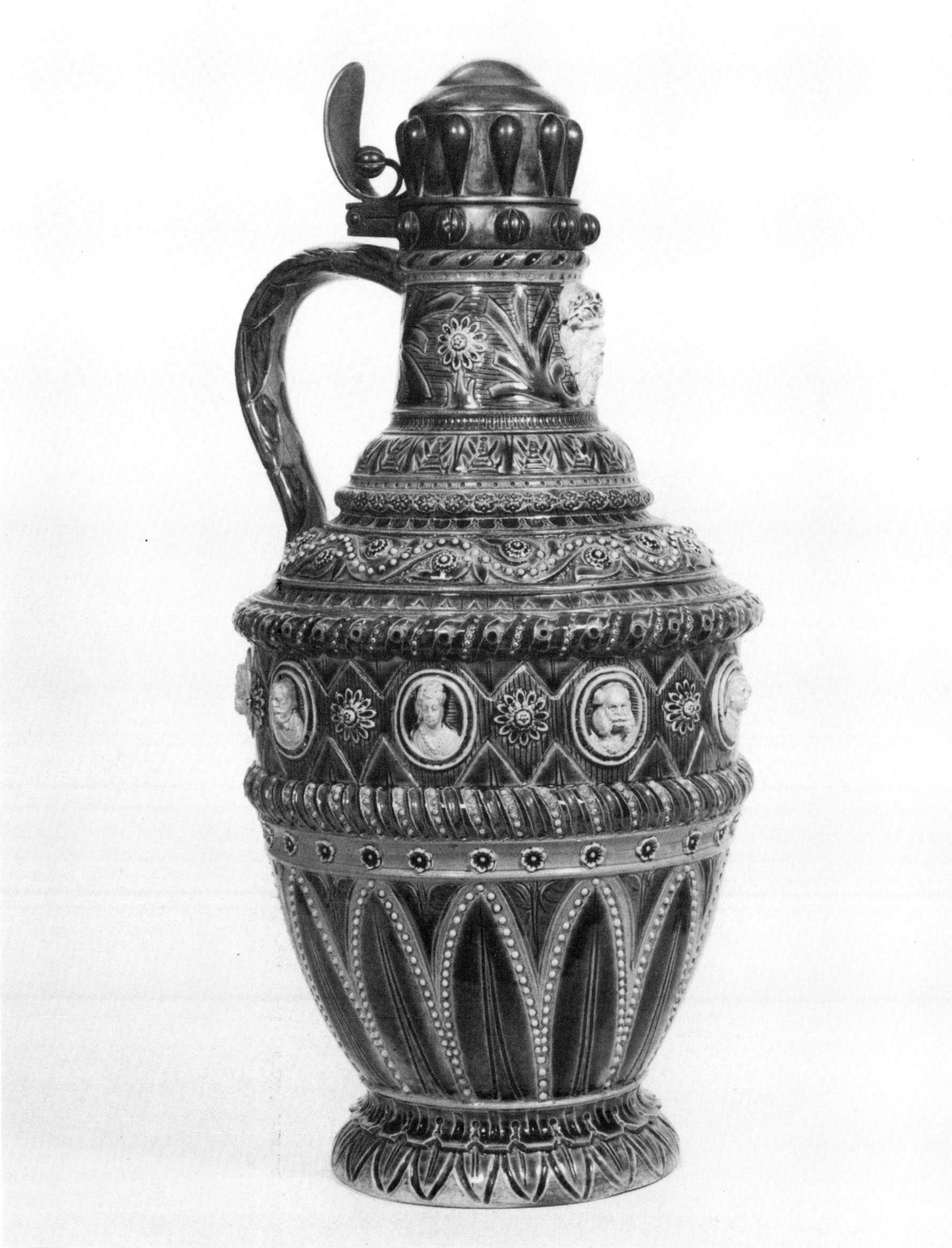

92. Jug by Arthur Barlow, with portraits of the King of Italy, Napoleon III, Queen Victoria, the Emperor of Germany and the Empress Eugene, 1873, 19½ in., metal mounts.
The portraits attributed to George Tinworth.